The Shotgun House and Other Stories

A Memoir

Michael B Kirkland

Dedication

To   Mama and Daddy,
       Matt and Regina Kirkland
       Sister Jean and Brother Matt
       With Love

And the Memory of all Family Members Who Have Passed, Most Recently, First Cousin Henry Deas Simpson III.

"Those we love are with the Lord, and the Lord has promised to be with us. If they are with Him and He is with us, they cannot be far away."

Peter Marshall

Table of Contents

The Shotgun House-Part I

"The past is never dead. It's not even past."
William Faulkner, *Requiem for a Nun*

I lived the first 14 years of my life, from 1938 to 1952, in a house at 312 Labauve Street in Plaquemine, Louisiana. Located about a block and a half from the levee and the Mississippi River to the east and about the same distance from the railroad tracks to the west, I remember growing up there as a child.

The family home was a white, clapboard frame structure with tin roof, open front porch, concrete pillars on either side of the steps, and a small screened-in back porch. A wall divided the house separating three bedrooms on the left from a living room, dining room, and kitchen on the right. A small bathroom separated the front master bedroom and the middle bedroom. A hallway, also between the front two bedrooms, provided 4-way access and privacy to the bathroom, living room, and each of the two front bedrooms. A telephone rested in an alcove in the left front corner of the hall and when you closed all four doors the hall became a little room of its own. A bare light bulb with a pull cord shone when lighted from the center of the hallway ceiling. Because of its double-barreled configuration, Mama called our home the "shotgun house."

One of two front doors to our shotgun house gave access to the bedroom suite and the other to the living room/dining room area. Friends and family knew to knock and enter at the living room entrance; others would often try the bedroom front door, which Mama kept locked. But when a deliveryman, like the man from Kean's Laundry and Dry Cleaning, came by, she would patiently open the door and take care of business. A single door inside the screened porch at the back of the house gave access to the kitchen, the social center of our home. This was the most popular entrance to the house. Ours was an informal, backdoor society. People dropped by, often at mealtime, to visit or say hello. Nobody called in advance.

We didn't own the house, we rented it, and the landlord kept it poorly. The roof leaked and at times we had to place a pan beneath the spot in the ceiling where rainwater pooled and dripped. The peeling paint on the outside walls made the house look brittle and dried out. Once Daddy absent-mindedly dropped a smoldering match into a cardboard box of trash on the back porch. A fire ignited and the porch was ablaze. I don't remember whether we got help but with a garden hose and buckets of water we managed to put the fire out. It's a miracle that the whole house didn't go up in flames. The owners repaired the black and blistered walls. I'm sure they were none too happy about it.

The house had no central heat or air conditioning. In summer, a large window fan in the front bedroom drew cool air into the windows we kept open there and in the other bedrooms. Small, Westinghouse oscillating fans also helped us stay cool. The fans made a low purr as the propeller rotated back and forth. The soothing sound and mesmerizing motion made us sleepy. In winter gas-fired heaters in each bedroom helped us stay warm. We ignited the heater by placing a lighted match near the burner while opening a valve. This took coordination and sometimes more gas escaped than we wanted. My big sister, Jean, almost got asphyxiated from inhaling the gas. There was a fireplace in the living room but we used it rarely and only when Daddy was home. Once when he opened the flue a bird nest and several live baby chimney swifts fell to the hearth. We called the featherless swifts "naked jay birds." The kitchen, where the stovetop burners and the oven were on most of the time, was a cozy place.

The kitchen adjoined the dining room by a swinging service door like the ones you see in restaurants. More often than not we kept this door propped open. Another open doorway to the right front of the kitchen connected to the back bedroom, which my big brother, Matt, occupied with me. An icebox, later replaced by a Westinghouse refrigerator, stood in the corner between the backdoor and the bedroom doorway. An old stove with an oven and top burners stretched between the backdoor and the opposite corner of the room. A counter and sink lined the wall to the left below a window. There Mama could keep an eye on me when I was playing outside or spot anyone approaching the house from the side yard. A small cupboard, which we called a "pantry," filled with pots and pans, sat between the back corner of the room and the service door. When I was small, age 5 or less, I could crawl into the cupboard, close the door, and beg Mama to slip snacks through a narrow opening at the top. More often than not, she would indulge me with a cookie or a piece of fudge. Serious eaters, however, and visitors congregated at the kitchen table next to the right inside wall. The table seemed hardly big enough for a family of five, but you could always pull it away from the wall to make room for more chairs. Even when Daddy was home in the evenings and on weekends, Mama didn't spend much time sitting down at table with us. She always served us from the stove or worked at the sink.

We used the dining room for Sunday dinners and special occasions. A dark maple table and six matching chairs formed the centerpiece. When we needed more room for extra family and kids, a folding card table provided an "extension" to the main dining table. A large, black upright piano occupied most of the inside wall. Daddy's bass fiddle reclined in the back corner beside the piano. The room anticipated good food and entertainment. Daddy played the piano, often before dinner, mainly to relax and unwind. But his playing also entertained us—and anyone within earshot in the neighborhood. Two small sets of decorative open shelves lined each of the front corners and served as a semi-divider between the dining and living rooms. Mama filled the shelves with colorful vases and framed picture stands. Family and company easily shifted from one room to the other.

The family often congregated in the living room around a large, wooden Philco radio and phonograph console placed between Daddy's stuffed easy chair and the front door. Here we heard our favorite shows and recordings. Unfortunately, the console was in the shop for repair a lot of the time. A matching stuffed sofa on the inside wall and another chair at the opposite corner of the room completed the set. A multi-colored, heavy-duty, corrugated coir rug covered most of the wood floor. I spent hours sitting or reclining on that rug listening to the radio or doing homework. Often the pattern from the rug squares left imprints on my bare legs. When I was about 12, my big sister, Jean, taught me my first dance steps on that living room rug.

When the radio was working, we listened to the Philco console a lot. During the war, we followed the latest news, including President Roosevelt's fireside chats and even some of Hitler's fanatical diatribes. We heard play-by-play Major League Baseball games all summer long, college football games on Saturday afternoons in the fall, and New York Mayor LaGuardia's Sunday comic strip readings. We'd often spread the comics on the living room floor and read along with him. Some of our favorite programs were "Judy Canova" on Saturday night, "The Shadow" on Sunday afternoon, and "Jack Benny" on Sunday night. We caught "The Inner Sanctum," "Fibber Magee and Molly," and "The Great Gildersleeve" on weeknights. Mama had her favorite radio soap operas then as many housewives do on TV today. The Philco record player managed a stack of heavy 78-rpm platters. Glen Miller was a favorite. I remember forming a human "train" with other kids and dancing around the room to the "Chattanooga Choo Choo."

We set up and decorated the Christmas tree in the living room each year, usually behind the sofa in the corner opposite the dining room. We stood the tree in an empty pail or paint can filled with dirt and wrapped in red and green foil. Mama let us help with the decorating. I especially liked setting up the crèche nativity scene with the baby Jesus, Mary and Joseph, and the magi—the "three wise guys," I called them. On Christmas Eve we would hover around the tree singing Silent Night and other carols. Christmas was Mama's favorite time of year.

From his easy chair in the living room, Daddy liked to sharpen my pencils, clean and trim my fingernails. He carried a razorsharp, bone-handled pocketknife. He would spread a sheet of newspaper on the lamp stand near his chair and neatly shave the sides of my pencil near the end until the lead point had a fine edge. He always did a better job than I could do with my little manual sharpeners or even the wall-mounted, hand-cranked pencil sharpeners we had at school. Often he would sit me in his lap and inspect my hands. If my fingernails were dirty, he would carefully run the tip of the knife blade under each nail and pull the dirt out. Then he would gently hold each finger and trim my nails. He never once cut or jabbed me with his knife. His body warmth and steady breathing made me feel safe and comfortable as he worked. It was one of those unspoken tender moments we had that I will always treasure.

We slept in three bedrooms arranged in a row: the master bedroom in front, a middle bedroom right behind the hall and bathroom, and a back bedroom at the rear of the house opposite the kitchen. Mama and Daddy slept in a double bed (there were no queens or kings then) with a simple mahogany headboard and frame, centered against the back wall. A matching dresser with four deep drawers lined the inside wall alongside a small dressing table and mirror. Sash windows brightened the room. A large window fan occupied the front window the summer. This was our "air conditioning system." In winter, the window was closed.

The front bedroom was always a special place. Not only was it Mama and Daddy's room, but also when Daddy was away, Mama let us take turns sleeping with her. My guess is that Mama needed the company and at the same time wanted to share her affection equally among the three of us. But when there was an argument or some question about whose turn it was, I usually won out, the advantage of being Mama's baby.

As a baby I can also remember sleeping between Mama and Daddy as I took my milk bottle. Daddy would heat the bottle in a small pot of water on the kitchen stove. To test the milk he would squirt a small amount from the nipple onto the inside of his forearm. If it passed the test—neither too warm nor too cold—he would bring the bottle to me in bed next to Mama, then snuggle up to both of us. I felt so warm and secure that I soon fell asleep. At that point Daddy would probably put me in my bed. Once when I was still wide-awake I slapped my Daddy in the face for no apparent reason. He was quite angry but didn't punish me in any way. However, I don't remember spending much time in bed with my parents after that incident. In a way, we were all rivals for Mama's affection, even with our own father.

Daddy always slept with his wallet under his pillow—a habit he carried over from the many nights he slept in the woods with logging crews where theft among the workers was common. I thought this was just something a man did and when I grew up I looked forward to doing the same thing. Daddy had hunting rifles and shotguns, but never owned a handgun. Otherwise, he might have kept one under his pillow as well. My guess is that he was more fearful of the harm a loaded pistol might do to us kids, than from the danger of any intruder. For my part, Daddy was the biggest and strongest man I knew and I was confident that he would take care of himself and the family in any situation.

My sister, Jean, slept in the middle bedroom, the smallest of the three. It, too, had a double bed with the head against the wall and the foot toward the doorway to the back room. A large mirror on the door of a small armoire faced the room. On one occasion, our cat (we had many) dropped a litter of kittens at the bottom of the open armoire. Jean's room was very popular; we often used it to access the bathroom, the telephone in the hall, or Mama and Daddy's room. She had less privacy than any of us but never complained about it. Decorated with pinks and pastels, her room was pretty and feminine. I treasured the times she let me play with her there on special occasions, like Easter. I think that Matt and I respected her space and privacy. If not, Mama would enforce it.

I spent most of my time growing up in the back bedroom, the boys' room, of the shotgun house. My brother, Matt, and I shared a double bed there. I can't say that either of us liked that arrangement, but it wasn't until I was about 10, that we enjoyed the space and privacy of new twin beds. My bed, located in the right rear corner, faced the window that looked out to our next-door neighbor's carport. Matt's bed, near the inside corner of the room, faced the doorway that led to the kitchen.

I remember taking a bath in a galvanized steel washtub in the wintertime in that room. The hot water pipes must have frozen under the house and my parents had to boil water in a kettle on the stove and pour it into the gray washtub. I thought it was fun—a diversion from the routine bath in the bathtub—and made the most of it. The notion of bringing the rugged, heavy outdoor washtub indoors appealed to my sense of adventure. I don't remember Matt and Jean bathing this way and certainly not Mama and Daddy. Perhaps I was just the one most in need of a bath. I dried off and warmed my feet by a potbellied wood-burning stove that sat in the corner of the room. A gas-fired heater later replaced the stove.

I can also remember as a little child lying on a cedar chest in the right back corner of the back room and taking my milk bottle. The cool, smooth surface and the sweet, clean smell of the cedar seemed to enhance my pleasure of sucking on the warm bottle. I would often nap afterwards right there on that little cedar chest. A bottle-fed five-year-old was unusual even back then. My only guess is that Mama, knowing she couldn't have more children, wanted to keep me as her baby as long as she could. I didn't mind at the time but was embarrassed about it later.

Mama often worked at her little Singer sewing machine on the same side of the room in front of the cedar chest. There, when she had time, Mama would operate the manual foot treadle of the machine as she stitched and sewed our torn clothing. She was not only a seamstress but also an excellent mender—skirt hems and trouser cuffs being her specialty. I loved to watch the up and down motion of the thread on the spindle as she buzzed along. I was also fascinated by the bright-colored, silver spools of thread that were tucked neatly in little drawers in a shelf right below the sewing machine table. I would sometimes play with them but always put them back, respecting that they were Mama's tools and not my toys. She pulled a black vinyl cover over the machine when it was not in use and to keep me out of mischief.

Next to the living room, the back bedroom was our secondary entertainment center. A brown, wooden Zenith radio console played music and shows from a stand in Matt's corner of the room. The radio had both an AM and a short-wave band. In the mornings we listened to the "Dawn Busters," a news and music show from WWL in New Orleans, or Pappy Birge, a local DJ from WAFB in Baton Rouge. Mama listened to her favorite soaps in the late morning and early afternoon, too, especially when the Philco in the living room was in the shop, or simply out of convenience when she was working right nearby in the kitchen. The radio was on most of the time and in the background as we went about our daily routines. I learned and sang along with many of the pop tunes at the time. Frankie Lane was one of my favorite vocalists. In the afternoon after school and before supper I would "sweat it out" with "Straight Arrow," "Sergeant Preston of the Yukon," "Jack Armstrong," and "The Green Hornet." On Saturday mornings we would escape to *Grimm's Fairy Tales* on "Let's Pretend."

Matt liked to use the short-wave radio band on the Zenith to listen to local Ham radio operators, as well as ship-to-shore communications among the boats in the nearby Mississippi River. To expand our coverage, Matt ordered an antenna from a catalog and I helped install it on the roof in the back. We could then get broadcasts from the BBC, Radio Moscow, Australia, and the Belgian Congo. We were amazed at the range and fidelity of the little radio. We really felt tuned in to the world. Matt kept a log of all the stations we received, including call signs of local short-wave operators. He could even translate some Morse code communications on the ship-to-shore network. We both studied Morse and Semaphore in the Boy Scouts. Matt had mastered them pretty well.

On rainy days I liked to play in the right front corner of the back room opposite a closet. A strip of molding about six inches off the floor provided a ledge where I lined up shotgun shells that I took from Daddy's hunting vest hanging from a coat rack on the back porch. The shells were green, orange, and red—mostly 16- and 12-gauge. I would line them up like toy soldiers in rows on the floor and on the molding. Then I would shoot marbles at them with my thumb and forefinger until I knocked them all down. It was a mindless, relaxing game that kept me occupied, sometimes for hours. I am surprised that Daddy, a stickler for safety, let me play with his shotgun shells. Since he was never around during the day, perhaps he didn't know and Mama didn't see the potential danger. Once a marble hit the cap of a shell and the shell partially ignited, emitting a little smoke and the acrid smell of burning gunpowder, but the load of birdshot (I don't recall that any of the shells contained buckshot) did not discharge. The shell was probably too old. After that incident I decided not to play this game anymore.

The front porch was both a playroom and a window to the outside world. I loved to turn the porch chairs over, pull them together, and drape an old bedspread over them. Then I would go inside of my little makeshift house. It was both a place to hide, which I loved to do, and a place to play. I also liked to watch the rainwater gush through the downspout from the gutter on the side of the porch during a storm. In the summer thunderstorms were frequent and violent. The open porch may not have been the safest place to be during such times but I found it exciting. I felt exposed to the elements—the lighting flashed brightly before your eyes and the thunder roared in your ears—but thinly protected by the tin roof overhead. I could smell the steam as it rose like fog from the baking street. The front porch was an open-air room, as it were, that provided a sense of freedom and spaciousness while otherwise securely attached to the house. Facing due South the porch captured both morning and afternoon sunlight. In the dead of summer there was little relief from the still, steamy heat. But I loved it out there.

I learned at an early age to jump from one concrete pillar to the other across the porch steps. The pillars were about three feet high; the distance between them was about two yards. I was apprehensive at first, knowing even then that if I missed, I could hurt myself, but I made it on the first try. Afterwards, I got cocky and jumped across those pillars on a regular basis. It was a way of claiming my space by dint of my athleticism.

The front porch was a place for sedentary pleasures, reading, watching the rain or passersby on the street. It was also a place for games. My siblings and friends loved to play cards. One summer they closed the swimming pool because of a polio alert, so we all played cards on the front porch all day long. I learned to play Canasta, Old Maid, Fish, Poker, and Gin Rummy. I was never very good at cards. The cards became so flimsy and dog-eared they were hard to shuffle. Some had a distinctive nick or tear that would allow you to identify them in another player's hand.

We also played games like Battleship. On a sheet of paper we marked carriers, destroyers, cruisers, patrol boats, and battle ships. Each ship, according to size, had a set of squares, indexed by numbers and letters on the borders of the sheet. When it was your turn, you called out a letter and number, hoping you scored a hit on an opponent's fleet. If you determined a pattern you could destroy each ship. This was a two-person game that I usually played with Matt, and he usually won.

Major league baseball captured my imagination from an early age. I studied the box scores from the daily paper and recorded them in a small spiral notebook. It would have been easy enough to clip the pages and make a scrapbook, but I enjoyed the discipline and dedication of keeping my own record. As a result I became a local authority on current baseball statistics, rattling off individual batting averages, home runs, runs batted in, strikeouts, as well as team standings in both the American and National leagues. The Boston Red Sox were and still are my favorite team.

I collected autographed photos of major league baseball players. I would send a penny postcard to the home field of each player asking for his autograph. It was a painstaking process. I would meet the postman at the front porch to see if I got any returns from my requests. In those days we got mail twice a day, which I figured doubled my chances. My rate of return was close to 50 percent.

My brother, Matt, and his friend, Farrell, had a favorite pastime. The two of them would read books aloud together on the front porch. One summer they read *Huckleberry Finn*. Matt read the part of Huck and Farrell that of Jim. Sometime they took turns. They read with expression and animation. It was a great introduction to Mark Twain and perhaps his most famous work, which I would read on my own years later.

Sitting on the front porch on a hot summer day, you could anticipate special treats. Years before the Good Humor Man and his friendly truck filled with frozen goodies, "Jim the ice cream man" pushed his cart around town. The cart was filled with the latest offerings from the Blue Bird Ice Cream Factory, our local frozen dessert plant. Jim blew a silver two-tone whistle to announce his arrival at various stops. He was like the pied piper of frozen snacks and kids flocked wherever he went. Since his "route" was the entire town, roughly five square miles, you were never quite sure when he would arrive in your neighborhood. Our best guess was mid-afternoon but you never knew for sure until you heard that unmistakable sound from his two-tone whistle: "Too *too* toot! too *too* toot!, too *too too too* toot!" Jim was a wiry black man who wore a white shirt, pants and sneakers and usually a white straw hat. His cart was white, too. You could see and hear him from blocks away. I had three favorites: a strawberry fro-li-pop (a single popsicle; a fudge-sickle (a chocolate version of the fro-li-pop) and an Eskimo pie (vanilla ice cream covered in a chocolate shell on a stick). I only had a nickel or a dime to spend so I had to make a choice; usually I did in advance.

As a break from the heat or one of our long, drawn-out card games, Mama would often surprise us with a summertime favorite called "ping-pong." Ping-pong was simply an ice tray filled with a pink, nectar flavored liquid that when frozen made a delicious summertime treat. Two trays of ping-pong provided enough cubes for all of us. Mama froze a toothpick in each cube that served as a "handle" when licking the treat. I hoped that this occasion also provided Mama a break from her busy housekeeping routine.

When our friends came to visit in the summer, we congregated on the front porch. As a young teenager, Matt was very popular. Boys all over town came to visit him. Matt was bright and competent in a quiet, understated way, but he was not particularly gregarious or outgoing. So I began to wonder: what was the big deal? Jean, at 13, was rapidly becoming a beautiful and physically mature young woman.

She never went through that awkward pre-adolescent phase. Her maturation was almost transparent. Although Matt's visitors stayed in his company, when Jean came out on the porch in shorts and a summer blouse, there was a pause in the conversation as they all took a collective deep breath. Every boy I knew from my age through Matt's had a crush on Jean. So did I. It was impossible not to.

All was not fun and games on the front porch. My first and most beloved dog, a beautiful six-month-old Collie, named Prince, died there. Pet care was minimal in those days. People didn't bother with shots, immunizations, and registrations. I doubt if there was even a local vet. We gave our pets love, food and shelter; otherwise the animals were on their own. In his case, Prince liked to roam away from home and we often had to retrieve him when he was "lost." On one such occasion he must have picked up a virus or an infection because he was quite sick. One night I heard him slowly pacing back and forth on the front porch, his paws tapping loosely on the wooden floor. Then the pacing stopped and I heard a dull thump. Half asleep myself I hoped that perhaps Prince had gone to sleep, too. But the next morning Mama told me that Prince had died and that Daddy had buried him behind the levee while I was still asleep. Mama explained that Daddy wanted to spare me the grief of seeing my dead dog. Prince was almost full grown.

The screened back porch, on the cooler, shady side of the house, was more functional than social. Daddy's hunting vest and hat hung from a rack in the right corner just above his laced, "Lil' Abner" work boots on the floor. I loved to play the man by lacing and unlacing those boots, not that I could go very far in them. Only Daddy could move in them with ease.

As a small child I would help Mama peel fresh vegetables on the back porch. She bought the vegetables from a farmer who made his rounds in a horse-drawn cart, announcing his latest offerings: "I got corn, sweet potatoes, black-eyed peas, lima beans, radishes, and turnips," he would shout. There was almost always something on his cart that Mama needed. I loved to strip the peas and beans of their skins and dump them into a tin bowl. The vegetables and the bowl were cool to the touch and I enjoyed an almost sensuous feeling as they collected. When Mama declared that enough peas and beans had accumulated, I was usually rewarded with a treat like a homemade cookie.

The back porch was also the scene of another summertime ritual: eating watermelon and having your face "washed" with the clean rind. My grandmother's maid, Maud, a sweet but brusque colored woman, gave me my first initiation. After I finished eating a generous slice of watermelon, she unceremoniously took the empty rind and scrubbed it across my face. She was none too gentle and I was a little hurt that she would treat me that way. Otherwise she was always kind to me. She and Mama laughed and explained that it was all in fun as part of a long-standing tradition. My face scrubbing was like an initiation.

Sounds

Living in a tin-roofed frame house with open windows in the summertime, we were surrounded by a cacophony of sounds. From a nearby landing, a small ferryboat carried automobile passengers across the river, usually every hour on the hour. The ferry would sound a warning whistle five minutes before departure. If you were not already on the levee ramp to the boat landing when the whistle blew, the chances were slim that you would get on board. Even when you were on time, the 12-car ferry was often full and you had to wait another hour to get to the east bank of the river. But as a child, the boat whistle was comforting in its resonance and regularity. You could pretty much set your clocks by it. Oil tankers also plied the river sending fuller, deeper sounds from their whistles but with far less regularity.

Freight and passenger locomotives whistled through town day and night. Some of them seemed to go on forever. You could hear their whistles as they approached town from the south, warning locals to stay clear of the crossings. In turn, a clanging bell signal would ring at the crossings, as the warning lights flashed while the gates closed. We could hear all of this noise from home as the windows shook and rattled in our little house. I especially liked to hear the whistle of the 10 pm passenger train that sped through town each night. Like that of the ferryboat, the train's whistle gave me a sense of closure at the day's end. I would also fantasize about being a passenger on the train traveling to parts unknown. Trains have always held a romantic interest for me.

The whistle at the Milly plantation and sugar mill that sounded like a foghorn at the beginning and end of each workday could be heard all over town. Its regular deep-throated sound punctuated our lives. The whistle also served as a fire alarm. A code was devised to associate a series of blasts from the whistle with a local landmark, like the city hall, the courthouse, or a major street intersection like Main Street and Railroad Avenue (near the train depot). A dark red, cast iron fire alarm box mounted to a telephone pole at each major intersection was used to trigger a signal to the firehouse. I assume that the fire chief, in turn, telephoned the mill to sound the whistle alarm for the appropriate code. The code was a series of whistle blasts—for example, 3—in short succession followed by a pause of about five seconds, followed by another series of blasts—for example, 4—indicating 34. Each home and business had a paper key to all of the codes, but since there were so few, probably less than twelve, it wasn't too hard to translate the codes from memory. Matt was always best at doing this. We could actually make a game of it and test each other's memory that way. But it was serious business, and often the sounds of the fire engine sirens clashed simultaneously with the sugar mill whistle while dark smoke billowed ominously from the site of the fire. I remember three major fires in town most vividly: the parish court house on Railroad Avenue, the Osage Theater on Court Street, and Blanchard's Cleaners next to the church on Main Street. In each case the fire spread so rapidly not much could be salvaged, despite the valiant efforts of our firefighters.

When it rained, especially during an electrical storm, you felt as though you were being bombarded by heavy artillery. The lightning flashed sometimes so close by that you could see and smell the sparks. Then the thunder would roar down as though the roof had just received a direct hit. And the rain pelted the roof like machinegun fire and we wondered how our little house could withstand such a violent attack. Sometimes Mama would light a holy candle and we would say Hail Marys, praying that God would spare us. But overall I liked the rain, strangely feeling protected in a house where security was fragile at best.

But one night I heard a loud banging on the roof just above my bed in the back room. I was frightened. I thought there was an intruder trying to come down from the roof and through one of the windows in the back room. I ran to get Daddy, woke him and told him what I thought was going on. Daddy calmly got up and went outside with a flashlight. There he found and rescued a cat who had got up on the roof and panicked when it couldn't find a way back down. I felt a little silly and ashamed that I woke my Daddy for that.

We were a noisy family, I suspect, though none of our neighbors ever complained about us. My own mouth was usually running at full volume most of the time. I liked to tease Jean and taunt Matt and when they reacted I usually got the worst of it. Mama, though normally quiet and soft-spoken, would sometimes throw up her hands in frustration when we got unruly and give us a well-deserved tongue-lashing. Anyone within earshot of the house could have heard. But I suppose that was considered normal dynamics for a healthy, growing young family.

Music was integral to our lives. Daddy played piano at home and a bass fiddle on occasional gigs with a local band. He also had a beautiful tenor voice and sang in the church choir and at weddings. He played by ear and was self-taught. When he got into a groove, he was a joy to listen to. Boogie-woogie tunes were among his favorites: "Dark Town Strutters Ball," "Beat Me Daddy, **Eight to the Bar**". He also reveled in blues like "St. Louis Blues" and others. His tastes were eclectic, however, and he often picked up popular tunes that he liked, bought and stored the sheet music to some in the piano bench. But when he was on a roll the house rocked and the neighbors on the block could not remain indifferent. Once when the Spedales, our neighbors across the street, were having a party, Daddy's playing caused such a distraction, they invited him over to play for them. As I recall he graciously declined. Daddy played for himself and his own enjoyment and was happy when others enjoyed his music, too; he did not like to play on demand or by special request.

All of us kids took piano lessons and played other instruments in the school band. Jean went further with the piano and Matt excelled with the trumpet. He would practice in the afternoons and evenings but even with a muted horn I'm sure his sounds carried throughout the neighborhood. I didn't get very far with the piano but faked my way fairly well with the slide trombone in the school band. I didn't practice much at home, however, so my neighbors were spared.

Home Deliveries

Mama relied on home deliveries at the shotgun house. She did not drive and we had no second car. Daddy drove his car to work every day. In the old days a horse-drawn ice wagon came down the street early in the morning, the familiar clop-clop-clop of the horse's hoofs resonating in my ears. From my bed I mimicked the sound by clicking my tongue at the roof of my mouth. I must have been just a baby because we soon replaced the old green icebox with a new refrigerator. We still called the new appliance "the icebox."

Mama ordered most of our groceries by phone from Kinberger's, our nearest neighborhood grocery store. Once a week she would call either Edwin or William Kinberger and place her order from a list she had compiled. I enjoyed hearing her recite each item as though she was sharing her wishes with a friend or neighbor. Later that same day a grocery delivery boy arrived on a bicycle with a large grocery basket attached. The basket contained large paper bags full of groceries. The grocery boy then carried the bags into the kitchen where Mama unloaded the contents and checked the items off her list. She would settle her account with the Kinberger brothers later that week or at the end of the month. Mama scrupulously managed household accounts. Looking back, this whole process seems vastly superior and more efficient than shopping at our modern supermarkets.

We also received home delivery of fresh milk from a local dairy. The milkman would leave a week's supply of whole milk in quart-sized bottles on the back porch near the kitchen door. Before homogenization, about 2-3 inches of cream collected at the top of the bottle. We kids didn't like the taste of cream and tried to filter out any chunks that poured out onto our cereal. But when he was home, Daddy would scoop out all of the cream from the top of the bottle into a bowl, smother it with milk and sprinkle crackers over it. He enjoyed this treat for breakfast or as an appetizer before dinner. Without the cream, he would break crackers over a glass of milk and eat the mixture with a spoon. Daddy so loved his milk.

Mama and our colored maid, Mildred, did the household laundry, but Mama relied on Kean's Laundry and Dry Cleaning services for dresses, skirts, sweaters, and Daddy's suits. Once a week the Kean's man stopped at the house, usually at the front porch door to the master bedroom. There Mama would take in the freshly cleaned garments in exchange for the ones needing service. Since we were on his route, Mr. Dawson or Mr. Pourcieaux would stop by to check whether or not we had any business for him.

The Standard Coffee man, Carlton Bourgeois, made regular stops every other week at the shotgun house. Carlton was a jovial, heavy-set man whose presence seemed to fill our small kitchen. We relied on him for our coffee perhaps more out of convenience than we did for a more popular brand, Luzianne, which was available at the local grocery stores. Again, I'm sure that convenience and Mama's strict accounting skills had a lot to do with it.

Street vendors like Jim the ice-cream man, the farmer in his vegetable cart, jobbers like scissors sharpeners, and seasonal river shrimp boys hawked their wares and services—all made available from the street or back door. Otherwise, right at the corner Rinaudo's served as our local convenience store. I ran errands there for Mama when we were low on milk, bread, or butter. The accessibility and availability of the basic necessities was rather remarkable.

Outside

I always wanted to go outside—in all kinds of weather. I loved to go out and play. In anticipation of spring, I would ask Mama each day when I could go out and run barefoot in the grass—the ultimate outdoor sensation. If spring had arrived but was raining Mama hesitated to let me go out. We would sometimes reach a compromise by my wearing shoes and raingear and promising to try not to get wet. But that promise was hard to keep because I loved playing in the mud puddles where I sailed my little paper boats. Mama couldn't believe how I could get so wet. Exasperated, she would say: "If a drop of rain fell from the sky, it would fall on Michael's head."

Outside of the shotgun house, my little playground consisted of the backyard, the shed, and the side yard. There wasn't much of a front yard to play in—just a little patch of grass between the front porch and the sidewalk. Often, as I grew older, the street itself extended the range of our games. This was my outdoor universe where the only limit to my adventures was my imagination.

My earliest memories of the outside are of me as a baby sitting on the front sidewalk and crying over my lost

Porky Pig rubber toy. (Mama took a picture of this scene.) The toy was my favorite and somehow it rolled into the street and down into the storm drain. Daddy managed to pry open the lid of the drain and retrieve the lost toy. After that Porky Pig stayed indoors.

I also remember riding my tricycle up and down the sidewalk in front of the house. I found the sensation of speed, control, and freedom of motion exhilarating. Soon I was bold enough to ride west to the corner at Eden St. As I gained confidence, I kept extending myself until before long I was able to ride completely around our block. It was a small block with only a few houses on each side but I considered it quite an accomplishment. Also, it extended my universe. I was never tempted to try crossing the street at an intersection and promised Mama faithfully that I would never do such a thing. Ours was a quiet neighborhood with light traffic but not safe for a child on a tricycle to navigate the streets. I would always report to Mama each time I made the loop both to let her know that I was back and to receive her praise, which she never failed to do. I soaked it up. My little "trike hikes" became my favorite outdoor activity until I gradually outgrew them and graduated to a two-wheeler bicycle.

The backyard was a narrow strip of land about 12 feet deep that spanned the width of the house and perhaps another three feet beyond. An old, bare L-shaped picket fence separated our space from our neighbor's, the Fryouxs (free use). Mr. Fryoux was a prolific gardener and urban farmer. He shared a fig tree whose branches spread over the back corner of the fence. The figs that grew on our side of the fence were ours for the picking. In the spring and early summer the figs turned a luscious golden brown, with faint tinges of purple. We could pick a small bowl full of them and bring them inside to have with our breakfast. We would peel back the skin and slice the fruit of the fig over our breakfast cereal. It was always quite a treat. Beyond the back fence, Mr. Fryoux grew a variety of vegetables: turnips, melons, beans—even corn. His crops were bountiful and beyond the needs of his family. He may have sold his produce to a local market. I'm not sure.

I would sit on an old bench under the overhanging fig tree and while away the time on an otherwise hot and sultry summer day. The bench was a relic from my grandmother's childhood plantation home. One July I carved the date with my pocketknife on the bench and did the same thing the following year on exactly the same date. Something about the continuity of time and place while repeating that act appealed to me—I don't know why. Time seemed to barely creep by during endless summer days back then.

In addition to my pocketknife, I had a boy scout hunting knife and a hatchet. I was fascinated by the skill employed by some of my comic book and movie heroes in knife and hatchet throwing. I practiced at length in the back yard, trying to bury the blade of the knife or hatchet in an elm tree that stood at the other end of the yard in front of the shed. I varied the distance between myself and the tree, trying to factor in the number of revolutions my weapon made en-route until I was finally able to throw a "strike." I was not consistent but felt some satisfaction that I was able to do it at least some of the time.

Daddy made a small barbecue pit in the backyard with slabs of sheet metal and a thick wire mesh cover. In the summer he would burn charcoal in the pit and when the coals turned gray, he would cook chicken on the grill. I loved to watch him turn the chicken parts over as he continually basted them with a pungent solution of butter and vinegar. Once when he was away, Mama used the pit to burn some trash. Later she discovered that her diamond engagement ring was missing. After frantically searching in the house and kitchen without success, out of desperation we rummaged through the ashes in the barbecue pit. There amongst the smoldering newspapers we discovered her ring, with black smudges that were easily rinsed off. I was especially happy for Mama. The barbecue pit came into play on a less happy note later in my life at the shotgun house.

***

The shotgun house had a twin. Right next door to the left of us facing the street, another house, identical in style and configuration matched ours. Only the pattern was reversed, with the living room, dining room and kitchen suite on the left and the bedroom suite on the right. The intent may have been to ensure maximum privacy for the sleeping quarters. My maternal grandparents, Ma Ma and Pa Pa Delacroix lived there for most of my first 14 years. A single, tin-roofed wooden shed stood at the back of the side yard between both houses. Two large barn-like doors opened to individual carports from the center wall of the shed right below the gable. My guess is that when the houses were built in the late 1920s or early 1930s the shed was intended as a two-car garage with one space for each occupant of the homes. But we rarely used our "garage" for that purpose. Daddy preferred to park his car in the side yard in front of the shed, always leaving enough space for parking in the adjacent yard.

The roof of the shed sloped gently away from the gable. On either end of the lowest part of the shed a doorway opened to a small room used for outdoor storage and work. The room also sheltered numerous animals, mostly cats, and an occasional dog. We accessed this section of the shed from the backyard. A faded dark green distinguished this section from the rest of the shed that was totally devoid of paint—not even peeling whitewash. Inside an old linoleum rug loosely covered a dirt floor. In the old days our maid, Mildred, washed our laundry with a washboard and tub (the same tub sometimes used for my bath) in that little shed. I remember watching her scrub each piece vigorously on the washboard as the water foamed with soapsuds in the tub. Then she would rinse and hang them out to dry on a clothesline in the backyard. Later we got a washing machine with an overhead wringer that we thought was quite modern at the time. Mama hated it—sometimes you could get your hand caught in the wringer—and you still had to hang the damp laundry out to dry. But somehow she and Mildred managed.

The dark recesses of the shed were the perfect place for games. It made a neat hideout for bandits or for action heroes in disguise. Captives could be locked away from their friends and families. Gold and loot could be hidden. It also provided an operating room for kids playing doctor. I remember playing the part of the surgeon, twisting a screwdriver on the bare tummy of my friend, Judy, my willing patient. The activity aroused me but I didn't know why.

The shed provided outdoor storage for a variety of things, like lawn tools and outdoor toys and bikes. I also used the shed to store a snake that I killed behind the levee. I put the snake in a large jar that I filled with alcohol. I then placed the jar on a shelf and there it sat like a specimen in a museum. The thick coils of the snake seemed magnified through the glass of the jar, making my trophy even more impressive. The snake remained in the shed for some time until the jar was accidentally cracked open and the smelly alcohol began to leak. With some encouragement from Mama, I got rid of the mess.

From the elm tree in the back yard I could climb up and onto the roof of the shed where I engaged in many imaginary adventures, stimulated by my proclivity for comic book adventure heroes and movies. I was Tarzan, swinging on vines through the jungle to rescue a friend or fight an enemy. I was an Indian warrior searching for a missing tribesman, a caveman (I read Alley Oop) battling a saber-toothed tiger. I usually played the role of the hero unless my imaginary villain had overwhelming super powers and therefore was "the greatest of all evils." Although I had friends and cousins, I played alone a lot—especially when Matt and Jean were at school—entertained by the larger than life creations of my mind.

Typically, on one of my make-believe adventures, I would climb over the hot tin roof of the shed and down the slope to the other side. There in the fork of a large, shady camphor tree I would talk to Maud, my grandparents' maid and housekeeper. I could barely see the outlines of her black face through the screened window above the kitchen sink. Often only the glow from a gold tooth revealed her presence. But she would talk to me and sing to me good-naturedly as I sat in the tree, regaling me with "'Possum in the 'simmon tree," and other favorites. She called me "Michael Henry"—why, I'm not sure because my first cousin Deas was named Henry Deas. Anyway, sometimes she would offer me a treat. "Henry," she would say. "Do you want some stale cake?" I would always answer in the affirmative. She would then laugh and say "Ha! That boy will eat anything!" I gathered that I saved her a trip to the garbage can. Maud and I had good times. She also convinced me that I could capture a bird by dropping a teaspoon of salt on its tail. Try as I might I could never get close enough to my prey to administer the paralyzing agent. I was a great source of amusement to Maud.

The side yard between both houses was my main playground for active sports, one-base cricket style baseball, touch and tackle football. I broke my arm when I was tackled during a game there, the first of two football injuries. When I played alone, I would practice punting the football over the telephone wires and into the street. I would also toss and bat a baseball at the telephone pole across the street, surprising myself when I actually hit my target. I liked these repetitive little exercises. Sometimes I would engage in a solitary game of catch with Matt or Daddy. Daddy let me practice my pitches, which often went wild, and he would have to chase after the ball. I always felt bad about that— not so much my lack of control but making Daddy run after the ball. But he didn't seem to mind and never complained.

Perhaps he thought that with practice I would eventually settle down.

The side yard was also the scene of games like hide-and-go-seek, no bears out tonight, and tag. Once we made a "telephone" with two tin cans and a length of string. I was fascinated by our ability to communicate on the device even though our little yard was no test of its range. In the summer, we would often get into our bathing suits and squirt each other with the garden hose. This was especially appreciated on days when the public swimming pool was closed. And it was nice to know that we always had the option of cooling off that way right at home.

When Daddy's car was parked in the side yard, we would often incorporate it into our games. The car itself would then transport our imaginations to exotic hideaways. On one occasion, however, Daddy left a loaded .22 rifle in the backseat of his car. Matt pulled the trigger of the rifle, sending a bullet through the car door and the wall of Ma Ma and Pa Pa Del's house next door where it smashed into the refrigerator before falling harmlessly to the floor. We were all very fortunate that no one was hurt. After that incident Daddy never left his guns in the car.

The street was like an extension of the yard in the sense that our games often took us out there—to run after a loose ball, to man an "outfield" position, to chase each other. In many ways it was better than the yard: long and narrow, you could extend the range of play from one corner of our block to the other. Traffic was the only obstacle and the momentum of the game would necessarily be broken by a passing car or truck.

When I was little, age 10 or less, the street was unpaved and filled with gravel (another source of play). Cars crunched by sending dust billowing up and descending on the house. Mama, a fastidious housekeeper, worked feverishly to keep the place clean. When the cars hit a loose pocket of gravel, little rocks would spray across the sidewalk. Daddy grew up in a world of unpaved roads and claimed that when he was a boy his feet were so tough he would run barefoot over gravel roads. Naturally I wanted to do that, too, but wondered when my feet would be tough enough to run over the gravel without feeling pain. An entire summer's worth of barefoot play didn't seem to condition my feet sufficiently. This was only one of several instances where I fell short of my Daddy's high standards. Not that he expected or demanded them of me; it was just that his example always seemed to be just beyond my reach. But it made me try harder and I sensed that pleased him. I wanted very much to please both of my parents.

When the city paved our street and all the other gravel roads within the town limits, I felt my life accelerated with the speed of my bike on the smooth almost velvety surface of the new blacktop. I was thrilled. A light powder left a white film there—a finishing touch that facilitated the drying of the tar and enhanced the smoothness of the surface. I glided across it on my bike and felt as though I was riding on air. My neighborhood and town were modernized.

The Shotgun House-Part II

The Neighborhood

For most of my first 14 years of life, my maternal grandparents, Ma Ma (maman) and Pa Pa Del(acroix), lived in a second, identical shotgun house next door. Their youngest son, my Uncle Lionel, lived there too until he enlisted in the Navy during WWII. Maud Dorsey, their colored maid and housekeeper, was also a regular member of the household. I learned from Mama that Maud was a teenager when she came to work for Ma Ma. She and Mama, who was the same age, helped raise the younger children in the family: Uncle Homer, Aunt Carrie, Aunt Ernestine (Beanie), Aunt Pamilla, and Uncle Lionel. Maud continued to work for my grandparents and stay close to the family well after the children grew up.

My memories of Uncle Lionel are fond but vague. I can only remember that he was good to us and that he played with us. Maud claimed that he buried some "treasure" in their backyard. I tried to dig it up but couldn't find it. In that case, I don't think that Maud was deceiving me. My guess is that Uncle Lionel, who had briefly gone to the seminary to study for the priesthood, might have buried some religious artifacts. Mama had a deep affection for Lionel, having helped to raise him, along with Ma Ma and Maud. She kept a picture of the smiling young sailor on top of the bureau in her bedroom. The picture bore a handwritten inscription: "Miss you—Love, Lionel." She wrote to him every week and waited anxiously for his letters.

I can remember watching Uncle Lionel as he dressed in his Navy whites in the back bedroom in preparation for his wedding. He was on leave from the Navy at the time. He and his bride, my Aunt Mary, were such a fresh young couple at the time, so full of hope and optimism. That is why it came as a shock when I later learned of Lionel's death. A neighbor child pulled me out of my first grade class at school to tell me that my Uncle Lionel had died in a plane crash and that I was to go home. It was a very sad day. When I got home, Mama and all my aunts and uncles (save Uncle Homer, who was overseas in the Army at the time) had gathered at Ma Ma and Pa Pa Del's house for mutual support. When I saw Mama sweep up my cousin, little Deas (pronounced dees), in her arms and hold him tight while crying uncontrollably, I sensed the magnitude of the occasion. Mama was trying desperately to hold on to life, to youth (Deas was the youngest grandson), as a beloved member of the family was leaving us. Even Daddy, who rarely showed emotion, wiped a tear when he came home. Lionel was like a little brother to him. It was a painfully hard day for all of us and my first experience with the death of a family loved one. It also brought home in a very personal way the impact of the war.

(I learned much later through research and family history that Uncle Lionel was stationed on Ascension Island in the South Atlantic. He was a radio operator on a PBY-5A seaplane that flew reconnaissance and bombing missions against German submarine activity in the area. His plane crashed during an operational mission from Wideawake Field, Ascension Island. During takeoff, the "port wing tip struck a vertical embankment on the left side of the runway. The outer eight feet of the port wing folded back, plane climbed the embankment and cartwheeled over onto its back." Rm2c (Radioman Second Class) Lionel H. Delacroix and four crewmen were killed.) Source: Terry pb-4y2@sbcglobal.net (18 Aug 2001).

Months later the Navy sent home all of Uncle Lionel's personal effects: a sea bag that contained his uniforms, civilian clothes, and underwear—even a pair of low cut white sneakers that still had grains of sand in them from the beach near where he was stationed. They also sent his hammock. Sailors always traveled with their "beds" and even though technically the hammock was Government Issue, the Navy sent it, too. I remember how we strung it up in the empty garage space of the shed and how we used to play in it for hours. The musty smelling thick canvas was quite durable and withstood the rough and tumble of us kids. Embraced by the folds of his hammock we also stayed close to our Uncle Lionel.

Finally, Uncle Lionel's remains were returned home and he was buried at our local cemetery. The honor guard and the rifle salute at his grave impressed me. I couldn't resist the temptation to retrieve some of the empty cartridges that were ejected from the rifles after they were fired. I kept them as souvenirs. The coffin, draped with a huge red-white-and-blue U.S. flag, was partially lowered into the grave. Then the honor guard carefully removed the flag and folded it into a perfect triangle. A naval officer handed the folded flag to Ma Ma. Normally the widow, in this case, Aunt Mary, would have been the recipient. My guess is that Mary, attempting to make closure with Lionel's death, wanted Ma Ma to have it. As sad a day as it was, Uncle Lionel's burial and ceremony was important for all of us in the family to make closure with his passing.

The War Years (1941-45)

We were all acutely aware of the war. Its impact was all around us: food rationing, tokens, metal and tin salvaging, synthetic margarine. Friends and relatives, like Uncle Lionel and Uncle Homer, who served in the military, brought the war home to us in a very personal way. Mama and Daddy listened to the radio broadcasts every night that kept us posted on the progress of our forces and the latest diatribes from Hitler and Mussolini. The newsreels and print media photos impressed me with the way the Italian dictator strutted around in his stuffed military uniform, his head seeming too large for his helmet liner. I would mimic him by marching around with my toy shotgun, wearing boot pants and mid-calf leather boots.

We were always looking to the skies, alert to the possibilities of invading aircraft. Huge blimps, dirigibles, floated by like puffy white clouds, regularly monitoring both air traffic and ships navigating the Mississippi. Like living near a military base, It was almost as though we were on a constant state of alert. Mama served as a volunteer aircraft spotter at our local courthouse. A narrow walkway encircled the marble dome of the courthouse. There, spotters could track and identify low-flying aircraft. About once a week and with no warning we would have air raid drills at night. A volunteer air raid warden, with hardhat and flashlight, would walk through our neighborhood blowing a police whistle and announcing that an air raid drill was in effect. It was lights out for everyone. The shotgun house was in darkness. Once I was caught in the bathtub during an air raid and had to sit in the lukewarm water until the all-clear signal was given.

Throughout this whole period, I felt the terrible presence of the war as a backdrop to daily life in our home.

But the real fears and dangers my parents experienced somehow made me feel safe and positive, that confirming our country's mission was simply right versus wrong, good versus evil, and we were the good guys. We *had* to win.

Nevertheless, when I learned that the war was indeed over, I was both surprised and overjoyed. It was not too long after we dropped "atomic bombs" on Hiroshima and Nagasaki, a reality I understood only vaguely if at all. Matt, Farrell, and I were at a Saturday matinee movie at our local Theater Wilbert. The movie stopped abruptly, the lights came on, and a voice from a loudspeaker announced: "Ladies and gentlemen, the war is over." A loud cheer went up in the theater and we all shook hands and slapped each other's backs. Then the theater crowd flowed out into the streets where automobile horns were blaring and people were hugging and kissing. By the time we got home, fireworks were popping as though folks had anticipated this moment for celebration. Our happiness was bittersweet, however, colored by the knowledge that Uncle Lionel would not be among the victorious troops returning home. I was seven years old at this moment, more than 75 years ago. I remember it like yesterday.

***

I would often visit Ma Ma in those days on the front porch swing of her house. There she would regale me with stories of her childhood and early adulthood. The gentle rocking of the swing caught faint summer breezes and the squeaking noise it made reminded me of the cry of a Redwing Blackbird. There Ma Ma would tell me how "it 'twas." Ma Ma had grown up in a large plantation home, called "Old Variety," down the bayou deep in the country. She described the conditions there in the latter part of the nineteenth century. To my innocent ears and vivid imagination, it all sounded idyllic. Her brother, my Uncle Charlie, was my favorite character in her stories. He was an outdoorsman, a hunter, trapper, and the official surveyor of the parish. His original maps of the plantations along the Mississippi remain in the parish archives. When Ma Ma was a little girl he would bring her songbirds, cardinals, and mockingbirds that he trapped in the woods. There, at Old Variety, he would build birdcages for his quarry. This fascinated me—the idea of bringing in a bird from the wild for domestication. Ma Ma told me that mashed potatoes and a variety of fruit was the mockingbird's favorite treat.

Ma Ma also talked a lot about her cousin, Michael Schlatre, whose exploits were both infamous and legendary. He survived the category four Last Island storm of 1856 in the Gulf of Mexico off the coast of Louisiana but lost his entire family—his wife, seven children, and nanny. Schlatre wrote a narrative of his experience that revealed his callous behavior toward his youngest daughter whom he abandoned in an effort to save himself, and his disdain for his companion, Thomas Mille, also a family relative, who was not strong enough to survive. Nevertheless, Cousin Michael returned home where he was regarded as something of a superman. He later remarried and raised another family on the nearby Enterprise Plantation. Cousin Michael was a religious zealot who on Sundays marched the whole family to mass in the morning and back to benediction in the afternoon. The distance to the church in town was at least two miles each way. At home he was a taskmaster, keeping his sons in the fields from sunup to sundown. When they were old enough to be on their own, all of them left him.

It was not clear whether Ma Ma was retelling these stories about Cousin Michael or whether she knew them from her own personal experiences. Regardless, she made her depictions vivid. I loved to hear her tell how "it 'twas" in the old days, and she loved to ramble on about them, as we moved slowly in the gently rocking swing. I loved to tell stories, too.

When I slept over at Ma Ma's house, she put me up in the back room where Uncle Lionel used to stay. After we said prayers she would inevitably break down and share with me her sadness about Uncle Lionel. Our eyes filled with tears as we cried and tried to console each other. Mama worried about subjecting me to Ma Ma's fragile emotions and asked her not to talk to me about Lionel, but I never stopped her.

***

My little universe beyond the shotgun house extended across the street to Rinaudo's store and its surrounding property. The store, a tall pale yellow wooden frame building, sat at the southwest corner of Church and Labauve streets. It was a combination grocery and dry goods store, with a little bar adjacent to the main entrance on Church Street. We used the store for pickup shopping like bread, milk, and cereal. It was our convenience store of the day. The proprietors were also our landlords.

From our front porch we could view the back of the store property that included a little garage right across from us on Labauve Street. We could also see the corner of the store at an angle where the dry goods section was located. The garage, which was open most of the time, revealed a dark red 1930s vintage Dodge panel delivery truck. The truck was mounted on blocks and was not used for most of the time we lived in the shotgun house. I assumed the vehicle was in disrepair but later learned from Mama that the Rinaudos had lost a son in the war and, in keeping with their tradition of mourning, would not use the red car. I found it all very mysterious.

Mr. and Mrs. Rinaudo were old first generation Italian immigrants who spoke broken English. Since there was a tax on practically everything we bought, both during and after the war, a penny was added to each purchase. For example, a five-cent candy bar was "sick-ity cents," (six cents) Mrs. Rinaudo would say. I soon got used to her jargon. I rarely did business with Mr. Rinaudo, who spoke even less English. My guess is that he maintained the stock on the shelves and ran the bar on weekends. In the old pre-war days he probably made deliveries to customers in the panel truck. The store and rental properties were managed by the two Rinaudo daughters, Tina and Anna, and son, Scott. Most of the rental issues were handled by Tina, the eldest daughter, and I believe it was she who informed my parents when the monthly rent went up from $35 to $40. Daddy and Mama made quite an issue over that. Tina was polite but cool and all business. Anna was sweet and feminine and seemed to like children. I don't believe either of them ever married. Scott's role in managing the family business was never clear to me. He was a friendly, athletic man who had pitched in the semi-pro baseball leagues. We kids stood in awe of anyone who had had any experience in professional baseball.

I don't remember how late in the day the store was open but Mama often asked me to run over and get a loaf of bread (15 cents) or a quart of milk (25 cents). If I had any loose change in my pocket, I would try my luck on the slot machines in the store. There were four of them as I recall: a quarter, dime, nickel, and penny slot. I was no more a gambler then as I am now so my slot of choice was usually the penny machine. If I won anything I would pocket the change. If not, I would cut my losses. I probably broke even. I especially loved to watch the colorful reels spinning inside the nickel machine when I played it. My pulse would quicken when ever so often two red apples and a purple plum plopped down *clunk, clunk, clunk*, in regular cadence before my delighted eyes and a sweet *ca-ching* rang out as five shiny nickels emptied into the coin tray. I'm not sure whether Mama knew what I was doing at the store, but when I returned from my errand later than usual, she probably figured it out. I guess it was okay with her if my gambling amused me so long as I didn't waste my allowance.

***

From the backyard of our shotgun house we could see across fields to the east the garden and backyard of the Neubigs. Their backyard extended beyond Ma Ma's but I'm not sure where it ended. I could look and sometimes see chickens feeding in the barnyard there. The Neubigs lived in a large, white frame house that was right around the corner on Church Street. They were a large family: Mr. Phillip Sr., Mrs. Olga, Phillip Jr., Lee, Mary Olga, Henry, Annette, and Jerry. They were very religious. Mr. Neubig often served mass when we were short of altar boys. Phillip Jr. and Lee went to the seminary as young boys but dropped out later. The boys were all older than us. They were talented, athletic, and spent a lot of time working with their father in his carpentry shop located farther up the road off Church Street. My sister, Jean, and Annette were classmates. Jerry, the youngest daughter, was a year older than me and was an occasional playmate.

Although our families didn't socialize, the Neubigs were always friendly to us. They called me "Mickey"—a nickname I acquired as a child but one that was rarely used by anyone else. On the one hand, I felt it was a term of endearment and affection. On the other, one of my pretty girl classmates was also nicknamed Mickey and I was a little uncomfortable being called a girl's name. This was before Mickey Mantle broke into Major League Baseball and who could have been more masculine than the great Mick.

I remember playing with Jerry in the Neubig's backyard. We would hang by our legs upside down from a chinning bar and talk to each other as the blood rushed to our heads and blushed our faces. Sometimes if we had two nickels we would each buy a Dr. Nut soda at Rinaudos and hide from the Neubig's maid, Susie, inside of the barn. Susie always wanted us to save her a sip and we were not very good about sharing.

I loved to play the game of Marionettes at the Neubigs. Jean and I would join Mary Olga, Annette, and Jerry for this uniquely Neubig game. I don't remember Matt ever joining us. Marionettes was another version of a puppet show. The stage, as it were, was the bedroom floor right in front of the bedspread. The marionettes, or puppets, would appear from underneath the bedspread. Their faces were pale skin-colored and painted with lipstick. Their "heads" were usually covered with colored socks and their garments were made from ribbons and pieces of sewing material. When the show began, two of our party mysteriously disappeared but I didn't seem to notice. The marionettes began to speak in tiny voices that thrilled me to no end. I was convinced that the marionettes were real little people who lived under the bed. Much later Jean and Annette showed Jerry and me how they drew little faces on the backs of their hands, dressed and hooded their forearms before thrusting their creations under and out from the bedspread for the rest of us to see. Jean and Annette or Annette and Mary Olga were the players/puppeteers in this little theater. Jerry and I were the permanent audience. It was a wonderful game of make believe that was totally engrossing.

Viguet's

George Viguet (vee-gay) ran an all purpose convenience store located up Labauve Street about one block to the west of the shotgun house, between Eden Street and Railroad Avenue. To call it a convenience store was a misnomer; it was more like a flea market. It was nothing more than a shed that extended from the rear of his house, a nondescript wood frame building partially obscured from the street. There were no floors in Viguet's little store. Old linoleum covered the bare, bumpy ground beneath. I'm not sure how rainwater was kept out of the store or what kind of drainage system, if any, was used. Inside the store thinly partitioned "rooms" allowed you to find anything from dry goods—shirts, shoes, boots—to sporting goods—baseballs, bats, gloves, hunting jackets, ammo for rifles and shotguns, and an assortment of used weapons from vintage Winchester lever action rifles to shotguns of every gauge and make. Viguet's wares also included a variety of foodstuffs with staples like bread and milk, soft drinks and sodas, candy and cigarettes.

Although Rinaudo's store was more convenient for pickup basics, we used Viguet's for out of the ordinary purchases. Viguet was a trader. Among other things, he bought and sold old books and magazines. In my late teens I foolishly sold him my complete collection of *Mad* magazines for 2 cents a copy! I also traded to Viguet a similar collection of *EC Comics—Tales from the Crypt, The Vault of Horror, Shock Suspense Stories,* and *Crime Suspense Stories*. Viguet probably sold them for at least 100 percent profit at 5 cents apiece. He always came out ahead on any trade.

Viguet, himself, was a character, famous for his slate gray flat-top crew haircut and brisk, aggressive sales manner. He would always greet me as "Delacroix," Mama's maiden name, noticing perhaps a strong family resemblance. Whether you had a specific thing in mind or were just browsing through his store, he would make sure you bought something. You never left empty-handed. Something was bound to catch your eye, then your interest, and with his help the object became yours. It was a sales trap, of course, that you willingly stepped into. If there was something you needed but couldn't find, the response in the neighborhood and around town was always: "Maybe George Viguet will have it." His establishment became such a hub of local commerce that a Greyhound bus station was posted there, ferrying passengers to and from neighboring towns and villages. What better place to rest and gather provisions for the traveling community?!

The Levee

The levee—barely a block away from the shotgun house —vastly extended my neighborhood. Our street, Labauve, terminated with Seminary Street at the foot of the levee. Living in a world that was perfectly flat, the levee was our only natural high ground, a green mound of earth that paralleled the winding Mississippi River to the north and south of town. It rose about twenty feet above the street and stretched almost the same distance from one side to the other. Cattle and horses grazed there. Wildflowers, daisies, black-eyed Susans, and clover abounded.

The levee was the closest thing we had to a park. We made sleds out of large flattened cardboard boxes and slid down the street side of the levee, gliding over the smooth, cushiony surface from the thick clover. In the spring, we would hike to the levee to gather clover in our Easter baskets and then make nests on the back porch for the Easter bunny to deposit his treats. Farther south along the river some communities would build huge bonfires on the levee at Christmastime. You could see them for miles away, lighting up the winter sky. One year, Daddy took us for a ride along the river road to see one up close. It was a beautifully dramatic and joyous way to celebrate Christmas and bring in the New Year.

At Christmastime we enjoyed the levee's heights to extend the range of our fireworks—especially Roman candles and skyrockets. We also shot a variety of firecrackers, 4-inch blockbusters, cherry bombs, and little grenades called torpedoes that exploded on contact.

One year my friends and I decided to liven things up and have a little war with our fireworks. We chose sides and began chasing each other with whatever explosives we had. Unfortunately, I carried my extra packs of firecrackers in my jeans back pocket. In the midst of the fracas, the firecrackers in my pocket started shooting off while I jumped up and down, frantically trying to brush them away from my body. I must have looked as if I were electrified. My friends were shocked. I was furious, thinking that my friends on the "enemy" side of the war had intentionally set the firecrackers off. When I finally calmed down, I concluded that amidst all the fireworks exploding around me, an errant spark must have set off the firecrackers in my pocket. Later, when I got home to assess the damage, my jeans pocket was completely blown off and my exposed rear end was black and blue from powder burns. We were young; the burns healed so fast I barely remember them. My pride was wounded, too, having made a laughingstock of myself.

We all agreed that this was no way for friends to behave toward each other. I don't remember if anyone else was injured or had provided as much entertainment for the group. Mama just shook her head in disbelief, probably wondering what other surprises Michael had in store for her. But I don't think anything else ever topped this one. I was about ten years old.

***

Once I reached the crest of the levee and descended its eastern slope toward the river, I entered another world. A wilderness replaced the cozy warmth and orderliness of the shotgun house. A narrow strip of swamp, thick with briars and underbrush, dotted with slender swamp willows, stood between the river and me. I no longer needed to fantasize about an adventure into the wild. Each step I took was an adventure. Narrow trails cut winding paths to the riverbanks; I made other trails myself by trampling the underbrush and cutting my way through the willows with a cane knife. But what at first was unfamiliar and somewhat foreboding, gradually, after repeated trips became better known; landmarks like an old stump, a bent willow, a shallow hole in the path, welcomed me back to a new adventure.

What did I do in back of the levee? Mostly, I played by myself. I stripped the tender bark off young willow saplings and made spears and arrows. With my BB gun, I picked off red-winged blackbirds singing noisily in the trees. Once I narrowly missed stepping on a large, black water snake, about three feet long, right in the middle of the path. I shot him in the head with my BB gun and carried him home on a stick like a trophy. There I lowered his coiled body into a large jar, filled it with rubbing alcohol, and placed it, like a museum specimen, on a shelf in the shed. I felt proud of my accomplishment.

At the riverbank, I marveled at the force of the swiftly moving Mississippi, roiling noisily with dangerous eddies—intimidating, even to an adventurous boy like me. I was in awe of its power. The river water was cold and muddy like creamed coffee. Even in the heat of summer, I resisted the temptation to drink from it. I never fished in the river, either, preferring more tranquil and cleaner waters in the bayou tributaries. But some folks caught river shrimp there and jumbo sized catfish.

Later, when I was in my teens and a fairly strong swimmer, my friends and I would swim a few yards out into the river, catch a sturdy piece of driftwood, float downstream a hundred yards or so, swim back to shore, and do it again. Mama knew that I played behind the levee but never dreamed I would be so reckless as to actually swim in the river. In my mind, what I did was nothing compared to my Daddy's feat of swimming a mile across the river at age 13! He set the bar pretty high for an ambitious youth like me. When I would come home after one of my adventures, Mama would ask: "Where did you go?"

"Oh, back of the levee," I would say casually. I could just as easily have been in a neighborhood park or playground—if we had had one.

My friends and I camped behind the levee on our own or with organized Boy Scout trips. But my individual forays into the wilds there meant the most to me. The sense of freedom and adventure was overwhelming.

***

The levee was the perfect place—the only place, really, to fly a kite. March or early spring seemed the best time, although there was no "season" for kite flying. Most of the kids made their own kites, eschewing the five and dime store kits that required some assembly anyway. I watched my brother, Matt, and his friend, Farrell make theirs with narrow strips of wood that formed a frame, heavy brown wrapping paper for the sail, all parts connected with a string and sealed with a homemade paste of flour and water. I was an enthusiastic observer but didn't yet have the skill to build my own kite. Once assembled, Matt and Farrell took their new kite to the levee for a test flight. Depending on the strength of the wind, which came up in gusts from the river, the boys would add sections of tail to the kite for stability. Rolled up newspapers, pieces of cloth, even small sticks could be used for this purpose. Sometimes you had to experiment because if the tail was too heavy, the kite would drag, too light and the kite would crash. I could help with that part of the operation and would supply the necessary materials.

Some boys liked to fight with their kites, making them light and mobile enough to steer them into an opponent's path. But this wasn't a good idea if one wanted to fly his kite indefinitely. Sooner or later the kites would crash and the game would be over.

One Saturday morning when I complained to Mama and Daddy that I didn't have a kite of my own, Daddy took me into the back yard and shed and made me one— from scratch. He pulled a loose board from the fence, split it into narrow rods for the frame, tied them together and connected the ends with kitchen string. Then he found some old wrapping paper in the house, cut it to fit the pentagonal frame and glued the paper over it with homemade paste. Next he made a bridle with string at the front center of the kite and attached a roll of sturdy kite string. Except for the tail, which he left to me, the kite was ready for flight. I was amazed at the speed and confidence with which my Daddy worked. It was like he did this all the time. Growing up as a boy in the country, activities like this were perhaps second nature to him. Short on patience but long on generosity and love, he shrugged off this accomplishment. I thought the kite was magnificent!

At my first opportunity, I took the kite to the levee for a test flight. Within seconds, after I ran a few steps with it, a gust of wind from the river caught the kite and began pulling it away from me in a southwesterly direction. I released the string from the spool as fast as I could but the kite kept the line taut, asking as it were for more slack to go higher. I could barely control it.

Then the kite started to zigzag and I began to lose control. *The tail*, I said to myself, I didn't put enough tail on the kite! I tried my best to pull it in, winding the spool furiously but the runaway kite would not heed my directions. Indeed, it seemed to have a dangerously erratic life of its own. Finally, after making a wild 90-degree turn, it continued to plunge downwards and crashed into the neighboring community below.

My heart was in my throat. I was devastated! On its maiden voyage I had sunk the Titanic of kites. Strangely, I felt that I was in foreign territory. The kite went down in a community that housed a section of Negro families. I had never been there before and never wandered into the segregated sections of town where colored people lived. The homes looked like tenement dwellings, shacks devoid of paint, separated by unpaved alleys. I was afraid but determined to retrieve my kite.

As I approached the community, I was met by a group of angry black boys. They held my torn and broken kite.

"Your kite crashed by my house!" one of the boys said angrily. "This ain't your neighborhood."

"I'm sorry. I lost control of it." Then as an afterthought, I said. "Did it break anything or hurt anybody?"

"You're playing in our yards with your kite," the biggest kid and apparent leader said. "You got no right— no business here."

"You're right. I don't. I'll go away. But may I please have my kite back?"

"This kite is ours now. We found it on our property. Now it's ours."

What did they want? I wondered. Why were they so hostile? Were they using my kite as an excuse to pick a fight?

Just then a tall black man, graying at the temples, came out of a house and walked purposefully toward the boys. "Give me the kite, son," he said firmly to the biggest boy.

His eyes still glaring at me defiantly, the boy reluctantly handed the kite to the man.

"Now you boys go on about your business," the man said, raising his voice slightly.

The boys gradually drifted away.

The man handed the kite to me. "Sorry about this and what happened to your kite," he said.

"I'm sorry it happened, too," I said. "It was an accident."

"I know," he smiled. "You go on and play now." Then he turned and walked back to his house.

Later that day I told Daddy what had happened. "You're lucky," he said. "The father sounds like a nice man."

"But why were the boys so mean to me?" I asked. "I didn't do anything to them."

"Colored folks have their property and we white folks have ours. We can't expect them to respect our property if we don't respect theirs. I know you didn't mean any harm but that's the way they took it. At least the boys did."

Frustrated and hurt I complained: "So what am I supposed to do—stop kite flying?"

Daddy smiled. "No, just try flying in another direction."

I thought about this incident a lot afterwards. My disrespect, though not intentional, was taken as such by the black boys. Why did it have to be this way, why this strict separation of the races? Before I confronted the boys, I was barely aware of their existence. If I had known them better, would that have made a difference? Probably not, I thought, because of the way things were. Besides, the kite was torn and broken beyond repair.

The year was 1948. I was ten years old.

The Spedales

Another world loomed right across the street from the shotgun house. The left side, back, and gardens of the Spedale home, a huge, turn-of-the-century, sparkling white mansion, with dark green shutters greeted us. Although the architectural style was late Victorian, the wraparound galleries (porches), high ceilings, lush, manicured gardens bordering high shade trees created an ambience that was southern to the core, not quite but reflective of the ante-bellum homes of a period one hundred years earlier.

Dr. Rhodes "Doc" Spedale, Mrs. Zoe, and Rhodes Jr. were our neighbors the whole time we lived in the shotgun house. Rhodes Jr. and I were playmates and boyhood friends. The contrasts between our homes and lifestyle were immediate and striking: conspicuous affluence and lower middle-class simplicity. For the most part, however, these differences were only on the surface. I was a regular guest at the Spedales and considered practically as one of the family. I even mimicked Rhodes by calling Mrs. Zoe "Mother." We were that close.

I was overwhelmed by the spaciousness of the Spedale home. On the ground level a two-car garage adjoined a utility room and passageway to a white-tiled kitchen. From the kitchen a swinging service door gave access to a dark, wood paneled dining room, impressive in its size and formality. To the right of the dining room a doorway led to a small den, where Doc Spedale sometimes met patients. The den overlooked a patio and the homes on our side of the street. Beyond the dining room, a large living room, with a grand piano, and an adjoining parlor occupied both sides of the home facing west toward Eden Street. But like our home, most of the guests and service people used the side and back entrances of the house to visit and conduct business.

A large, carpeted stairway between the den and parlor led to the bedrooms upstairs. The master bedroom occupied most of the front of this level. Just to the right and below Doc Spedale used another smaller bedroom when he was called out in the night for medical emergencies. A long, spacious bathroom ran between the master bedroom and Rhodes' bedroom at mid-level. At the very back end another bedroom and bath was available for visiting family and guests. Also at that end of the house an outside stairway provided a private entrance/exit like a fire escape. A long, dark red-carpeted hallway separated all of these bedrooms from one end of this top level to the other. The plush, multi-dimensions of the home, fascinated me. In terms of square feet, our little shotgun house could probably have fit within any two rooms in the Spedale home.

The grounds of the Spedale home extended from one end of the block to the other—from Eden Street on the west to Church Street on the east. A tiny white and green guesthouse called "the cottage" sat just beyond the back yard. A flagstone walkway, lined with lilies, connected this little house to the garage and the main house. Mama's brother, my Uncle Homer, and Aunt Virginia rented the house for a while after the war until they started a family and needed more space. The cottage was also a convenient place for kids' parties, sleepovers, and a place for us to congregate during grownup parties in the big house. Regardless of the occasion, Mrs. Zoe always insisted on naptime for Rhodes, and his guests had to follow suit. I'm not sure how much we actually slept but we put in the requisite time.

***

My first sleepover at the Spedales was aborted early in the night. I couldn't sleep, missed my Mama, and cried to go home. I was all of six. I remember running across the street in my pajamas and bare feet to Mama's welcoming arms. Just the idea of being separated from the shotgun house, clearly visible from the Spedales, was enough to make me homesick. Within a few months, I soon got over it though because the thought of spending the night in the palatial, storybook environs of the Spedale home helped me overcome my tender emotions. Each visit was an adventure. Stairs and stairways fascinated me. The idea of moving about from one level of the home to the other, each separate and distinct, was a novel experience, like living in two homes under one roof. The only other time I couldn't make a planned sleepover, I ran over to tell Rhodes that I had the chickenpox.

In the mornings and during all of our meals we ate in the main, darkly paneled, dining room, although there was a dinette table in the sparkling white kitchen. Mrs. Zoe's servants were already busy about their chores and served us at the formally set dining table. We could choose from hot or cold cereal, eggs any style, bacon and toast. Fruit and freshly squeezed orange juice was always available. I usually chose whatever Rhodes was having. Mrs. Zoe and Doc Spedale seemed pleased with my politically correct decision.

If I opted to spend the day after a sleepover, Rhodes and I would play games in the morning, lunch in the same dining room, and nap in Rhodes' room for an hour in the early afternoon. Naptime was followed by Rhodes' piano practice on the baby grand in the living room. I could either hang around for that or go home. If Rhodes and I had a plan, post piano practice, I would usually wait. Mrs. Zoe was just as strict about that as she was about naptime. One didn't even think about crossing her. I was impressed with both the formality of the music lesson and the discipline that Rhodes employed. It was like seeing another more serious side of my friend. Somehow I sensed that he knew and respected that the practice and performance of music was his calling even though the child in him wanted to go out and play.

***

Rhodes was diagnosed with tuberculosis when he was about seven years old. He was in the first grade and I'm not sure whether he actually finished because the Spedales arranged for him to go to a private boarding school in Tucson, Arizona, where the dry climate was more favorable for his condition. None of us knew very much about TB except that it was a serious disease that required the best of medical attention. Clearly, it was beyond the capabilities of Doc Spedale, a surgeon, and Mrs. Zoe, a former nurse practitioner. That impressed us.

I can remember clearly the day Rhodes left. I was eight years old in 1946. We all gathered at the Spedale home to say our goodbyes. Doc Spedale and Mrs. Zoe tried to maintain a positive attitude, focusing on the opportunities the school and locale would provide. Rhodes seemed full of anticipation for the new adventure that awaited him. We shook hands and promised to keep in touch. Then Mama's tears began to flow as she hugged Rhodes desperately. None of us knew how long we would be separated from Rhodes. Tucson, Arizona, seemed like a far away world to me.

Rhodes' farewell began a series of departures and homecomings as his western education became permanent. He continued his residence and schooling in Tucson throughout the remainder of his secondary education, coming home for Christmas holidays and summer vacations.

Long distance phone calls were a novelty back then. You would first place the call through your local operator who would in turn connect you to a long distance operator. That operator would ask for the number and location of the party you wished to reach. She would then ask you to hang up while she tried to make a connection with your party. If successful, she would call back and announce that your party was on the line. If not (the line as busy or the party was not available), she would ask if you wanted her to keep trying or to cancel the call. Sometimes, when the Spedales set up these calls to Rhodes, Mrs. Zoe would call me over and if the call was successful, we would take turns talking to Rhodes. I felt especially privileged because I knew these calls were expensive, and grateful that they were willing to share phone time. I guess they knew it was important for both Rhodes and me to keep in touch. But although I recognized his voice, Rhodes sounded so far away.

Homecomings were always special. There were brief periods of adjustment when we sized each other up—who had grown, what we had learned at school, what we were doing and, of course, girls. Mickey Supple, a classmate and friend, was one of our favorites. Blonde and blue eyed, Mama always said she looked like a little China doll. Rhodes and I thought she was pretty, too, but more of a buddy than a girlfriend. For reasons beyond me, we never carried that friendship to a higher level, although I'm sure we both had our fantasies.

* * *

Not long after Rhodes' first homecoming, the Spedales invited me over for dinner with them. They were serving meatballs and spaghetti, my favorite dish. But when I asked Mama if I could go, she said "No."

I was shocked. "Why?" I asked.

"I just don't think it's a good idea." She didn't seem comfortable with this explanation. "Besides, I was already planning dinner for us at home."

That wasn't good enough for me because I had spent a lot of time at the Spedales in the past before Rhodes left for Tucson and there was never any problem. Since Daddy was away I thought that perhaps Mama was feeling lonely. "I won't be long, and I'll come back right after dinner."

"That's sweet, Michael, but I don't think it's a good idea to go at all."

That "good idea" explanation was no reason at all for my young mind. But I was aware of the difficulty she was having. It seemed as though she was dealing with some inner conflict. She wanted to let me go but something was holding her back. But I kept pleading with her anyway, hoping to wear down her resistance.

Finally, Mama started to cry and held me close to her. "Oh Michael, I don't want to disappoint you because I know how much this means to you."

I had seen Mama cry in the past but never like this before. "But why are you crying, Mama? I didn't want to upset you." I was beginning to regret that my persistence had gone too far.

"It's not your fault, Michael. Maybe I'm just an old worry wart, but I'm afraid if you have meals with Rhodes you might get sick, too."

I was stunned. "You mean the TB?" We all found the shorthand easier to use when we were referring to tuberculosis. I never thought that one could catch that dreadful disease from someone else, not knowing then that it was infectious.

"Yes, Michael, and if you did, we wouldn't know what to do. Daddy and I couldn't send you away to boarding school." Her sobbing now verged on hysteria.

"And I wouldn't want to go!" Then I hugged Mama and tried to comfort her. We were sitting in the kitchen and as

I held Mama, I looked around the room with a view to all things familiar there, in the living room and the back room. All the things that made me feel comfortable, safe, and loved. And I realized how lucky I was and how much I loved my Mama. Then I began to cry, too. "It's OK, Mama, I don't have to go. I'll just tell them I can't. I'd rather stay here at home with you."

Then Mama began to sober up. "No, you go ahead. And have a good time. I just needed to explain to you how I felt."

Despite my protestations she insisted that I go and that she would be all right. Somewhat reluctantly, and with far less enthusiasm, I went.

The dinner was delicious.

From that point forward there was never any discussion about my visits to the Spedales or having meals there. Their's was, after all, a doctor's home where guests would never be exposed to anything contagious. But the incident showed a tender, vulnerable and perhaps too protective side to Mama, which deepened my love for her and brought us even closer together.

***

Originally a grassy driveway paralleled the main driveway at the rear of the Spedale property that adjoined the Rinaudos. The driveway extended beyond the cottage to another yard and a shed. There may have been a chicken house back there at one time. I remember seeing Leggo, an ancient graying Negro, the Spedale's all-purpose handyman, wringing the necks of two fat chickens, simultaneously spinning them around in each of his hands and then letting them flop on the ground, like fish out of water, as they died. I also saw Leggo decapitate a large rat with a hoe in that far back yard. His movements were slow but deliberate and always effective.

Much later after Rhodes was fully ensconced in his western boarding school environment, Mrs. Zoe, who had a penchant for both indoor décor and outside landscape gardening, planned a major transformation of the grounds and home. First, the driveway from our street, Labauve, was filled in and planted with colorful shrubs and lilies. A new shell driveway was built from Church Street and curved around to a new carport behind the original garage. The garage itself was at first converted into a recreation room with ping-pong tables. Later it was layered with an industrial green carpet, furnished with a wet bar, and named the 'bar-rage" by Mrs. Zoe. The oil stained bare pavement of the old garage was soon forgotten.

In the space where the old shed used to sit, Mrs. Zoe built a stable with three stalls. Three comely steeds soon inhabited the stalls: Mary Ann, a tall, elegant Tennessee Walker, Triple-check, a golden palomino, and Rain-check, her rambunctious colt. In the early summer evenings the

Spedales, resplendent in western regalia, would ride around town—Doc Spedale on Mary Ann, Mrs. Zoe on Rain-check, and Rhodes on Triple-check. It was like a colorful scene in a Roy Rogers western movie. All that was lacking was a serenade by the "Sons of the Pioneers."

The gated driveway at the Church Street end of the property served as both the entrance to the home and a paddock for the horses. There must have been another gate near the cottage to keep the horses fenced in when they were out of their stalls. Appropriately, a pair of Dalmatian stable dogs completed the picture. A stand of bamboo behind the cottage gave Mrs. Zoe the idea of naming this little ranch the "Bar Bamboo" while she was away on a shopping expedition out west. Unaware of her plan, Doc Spedale decided to clean up the area by removing the bamboo as a surprise for Mrs. Zoe when she returned. She was furious that this *surprise* had essentially scotched her idea and that Doc Spedale had intruded on her domain.

*****

Games. You name it, we played it when Rhodes was home for summer vacation.. Upstairs in Rhodes' room, we lined up rows of toy soldiers and waged war. We each had a large chunk of clay from which we plucked and rolled little balls and threw them at our opponent's forces. There were so many soldiers that often our battles spilled out into the carpeted hallway and even to the stairs. Mrs. Zoe, a fastidious housekeeper, would complain: "Clay, clay, clay! All I see is clay!" After helping clean up as best we could, she insisted that we continue our war games in Rhodes' room.

Weather permitting, outdoor games predominated our play on the vast grounds of the Spedale estate. Rhodes was obsessed with baseball, which he could play during the entire school year in Arizona and all summer long at home. Like me, he had an autographed photo collection of major league baseball players and other memorabilia. He even owned a baseball that was allegedly fouled off by the immortal Babe Ruth. Rhodes had a blazing fastball and wicked curve that was a challenge to catch. He was a tall, skinny, bespectacled kid with a mouthful of braces. But his pitching speed and power belied his lanky, almost frail appearance. Kids from the neighborhood congregated at the Spedales for a round of baseball. Sometimes we'd play in the yard adjacent to the garage, but the driveway/ paddock area near the stables was preferable. There we could use the white fence and gate at the driveway as our "centerfield" fence. With my little 32 ounce "Hanna" bat I could just barely clearly the fence for my home runs.

When we weren't playing baseball, the stables area provided an excellent setting for western adventures. As I recall, Rhodes would write a script for a western action movie. Friends and I were assigned roles and the entire episode was filmed with a 16mm camera. I don't remember who actually filmed the event because I'm almost sure that each of us, including Rhodes, had a part to play. After the film was developed, Rhodes would show the episode to friends at parties. This was our version of a home movie, which we thought was pretty sophisticated at the time. And I rather enjoyed the notoriety I achieved as a local "film star."

Rhodes also had a recording device that would allow us to cut our own records. He, Billy Wilbert, another friend of ours, and I gathered in his room. Vaughn Monroe's "Riders in the Sky" was a top hit on the pop charts at the time and I mimicked it verbatim, as I did all pop tunes that appealed to me. We called ourselves the Perfecto Unique Trio—P. U. for short—and after a brief rehearsal we were ready to start. We had barely got the words "An old cowpoke…" out of our mouths when the three of us began to laugh hysterically. It was almost impossible to continue singing it straight, but somehow, we managed to finish. Hearing ourselves during the playback was even more hilarious than during the recording session. Along with our home movies, our homemade recordings also provided entertainment at Rhodes' parties.

***

The Spedales loved to entertain and Mrs. Zoe's summertime western bash was one of their most memorable parties. Guests were encouraged to wear their jeans, boots, Stetsons, frayed leather jackets, wide leather belts with big silver buckles, and ornate jade bracelets and necklaces. Mrs. Zoe, setting the tone with her newly acquired western finery, could have won a "best dressed" award should there have been such a contest. Some of the guests camped it up by wearing gun belts with holsters and cap pistols.

The party included both adults and children. Most of the adults congregated around the patio, den, and the wet bar in the bar-rage. Tom Wilbert, one of the adult guests, assumed the role of bartender and began to freely pass out mixed drinks to us kids as well. Then we would steal over to the cottage where most of the kids had gathered. Mrs. Zoe went ballistic when she found out what was going on. I can remember her attempting to chase us down the path to the cottage, armfuls of her silver bracelets jingling nervously. None of us kids got drunk; it was just the thrill of participating in the grownup celebration that we enjoyed. All of the Spedale parties were great fun but this one was the most memorable.

Best Friends

Besides Rhodes I was blessed to have many friends, chief among them were my first cousins, Johnny Carville and Deas Simpson. Johnny and I were peers and started first grade together. Johnny was a fair, grey-eyed, tow-headed kid in contrast to my dark-skinned ruddy brunette.

We were about the same size and we played well together, lots of rough and tumble. We also exchanged sleepovers at each other's homes. Johnny's first house was a little brown bungalow at the northeast end of town right next to the levee. It was a cozy little home but as the family expanded the Carville's moved to a large, two-story frame house with a wraparound porch just a few blocks to the south of us at the corner of Fort and Eden streets.

Johnny and I shared a desk in the first grade at St John's Elementary School. There was no parochial pre-school or kindergarten. The desk was a rustic hardwood with cast iron fittings and an inkwell on either side of the top. Carved initials and dark ink stains from previous occupants gave the desk a well-used appearance. I remember the two of us trying to write the figure 8 that Sister Mechtilda drew for us on the blackboard. We did it by drawing two little circles, one on top of the other. We soon caught on, however, and began to write the number correctly. Johnny was very studious from an early age and took his assignments seriously, completing them all to the letter. I found penmanship especially challenging and hated the homework exercises that required me to write my name repeatedly in my tablet, keeping the letters evenly within the large lined rules. I complained to Mama: "I wish my name was Bob!"

Johnny and I competed as a team in a contest to "win" a "pagan baby," a school wide program designed to raise money for missionary work among indigenous people in the Far East. A score chart was installed in the back of the classroom where each team could track its progress. Based on our donations, Johnny and I reached the top of the chart first. But we were surprised and disappointed to learn that we didn't actually win a pagan baby after all but merely contributed to its religious education.

My cousin, Deas, was a year or two younger than me and in a way more like a little brother. We played together, mostly cowboys and Indian games, each carrying a holster with a little cap pistol. Someone took a picture of the two of us on the front porch of Ma Ma Del's house. We looked like mean little hombres. Deas was brown-eyed like me but not quite as dark complected, his hair a lighter brown. His build was husky compared to my wiry physique. Since his mother, Aunt Carrie, was Mama's sister, the two families, the Simpsons and the Kirklands, probably got together more. As a result, I probably slept over more with little Deas. I loved the hot summer nights when Deas and I in our undershorts would stay up late telling each other ghost stories until Uncle Deas would enforce quiet time. When we were very small Aunt Carrie would sing lullabies like "Go tell Aunt Rhodie" and we would soon fall fast asleep. Deas and I spent a lot of time hunting and fishing throughout our boyhood.

In addition to Rhodes and my cousins, I also played with classmates, most of whom came to visit at the shotgun house. Marvin Flatau, Alvin (Lou) Brown, Tommy Wilbert, and Billy Wilbert. I never thought of myself as popular at the time but each of those boys at intervals was thought of as a best friend. They didn't hang around the house just to catch a glimpse of Jean (although that was always a special treat); we spent a lot of time doing things together. And with our bicycles we were quite mobile.

I got my first bike, a 26" red and white Schwin from Tommy Wilbert. Tommy's dad brought it over to the house one afternoon and my daddy gave him ten dollars for it. That and a handshake sealed the deal. I was impressed by both the simplicity and the semi-formality of the transaction. Ten dollars seemed like a lot of money to me. I loved the bike and used it for many years thereafter. Although the 26" model was a little tall for me, I soon grew into it. Tommy advanced to newer bikes and later to motorbikes.

The Shotgun House-Part III

Schooldays

At age five, I had a burning desire to be in school. After all, Matt and Jean were already there and I sensed that all the action and fun happened at school. Mama gave in to my demands and decided to give it a try. The nuns insisted that I first learn my abc's. I may have been halfway through the alphabet, but I was simply not mature enough for first grade work. Mama and the sisters agreed that I should wait another year when at age six the adjustment would be smoother. They were right, of course, and practically all of my friendships at school stem from that very first year in 1944.

Everything was within walking distance of the shotgun house. Our school, St. John's elementary and high school and church, St. John the Evangelist, were just four small city blocks away—perhaps a quarter of a mile.

When we turned the corner at Church Street on the way to school, we faced the familiar Neubig home, with its white picket fence and wide and inviting front porch. Sometimes Annette and Jerry Neubig joined us. But directly across the street we faced an old two-story house that appeared to have been deserted. Huge, moss-covered live oak trees masked portions of the house, making it difficult to see a dedicated entrance. A rusty iron fence with a broken gate separated the house from the sidewalk and street. Most of the front windows were cracked and broken. The house was in total disrepair, either from neglect or abandonment. Except that a family lived there. We rarely saw them out front and suspected that their living quarters were somewhere in the rear of the building, out of sight of curious onlookers like me. Once in a while some of the occupants emerged: a little girl about Jean's age, a little boy about the age of my younger cousin Deas, and a strange old lady who wore a scarf pulled tightly over her head. They were not social, had little or no contact with the rest of the neighborhood, and pretty much kept to themselves. The children, we assumed, went to the public school. Shrouded in mystery, we called their home the haunted house.

Despite our fears, we sometimes crossed the street to walk in front of the old house on the way to school. In the fall the oak trees showered acorns on the sidewalks. We loved to feel them crunch below our feet as we walked briskly past the house, hoping at the same time to catch a glimpse of someone through the broken windowpanes. We rarely saw anyone, but when we did we were not greeted in a friendly manner.

Church Street intersected with Haase at the next corner on our route to school. There the back lot and white frame building of our local hospital, the Plaquemine Sanitarium, occupied the entire west side of the block. In our free time the lot became our playground for baseball and football games. Across the street the front yard of the Tircuit family bungalow teemed with flowers, plants, and a small vegetable garden that in spring featured a strawberry patch. As we continued to walk past the next intersection at Merriam Street, we sometimes saw icicles hanging from outdoor spigots in the wintertime. Often we tried to break off a piece and suck on it—just for fun. By contrast, the heavy fragrance from spring flowers—azaleas, hydrangeas—perfumed us all along the way. Other children—some less enthusiastic than others—from neighboring homes joined our little procession. When we reached the next corner at Church and Court Streets, the walls and buildings of our school appeared.

The school was originally the site of the Scratchley mansion, an antebellum home built near the river in the 1850s. It was later leased to the Mariannite order of nuns and became a convent. The sisters converted parts of the frame building into a school, St. Basil's Academy in the early

20th century. Mama graduated from St. Basil's. The school later became St. John's, probably to reflect the parish and the church of St. John the Evangelist.

Sister Mechtilda taught first grade to me and my peers, Matt and Jean, and just about everyone else I knew who had attended school at St. John's. She was a short, plump, rosy-cheeked little nun with a cheerful disposition. She wrote our lessons and assignments on the blackboard while turning to the class to see if we understood. She moved about briskly while exhaling through her teeth, making a hissing sound. I'm sure we gave her cause but I never saw Sister Mechtilda get angry or lose her temper. She could enforce discipline simply by declaring and standing by the rules, which we all grew up to recognize and respect.

Besides Sister Mechtilda, the classroom, the playground outside, and the grotto of the Blessed Virgin Mary made lasting impressions of the first grade. The convent (the nuns' quarters) and classrooms were built in the shape of an open quadrangle with the first grade opposite at one end from the other grades on the other. About sixty first graders sat in double-occupancy desks in one large classroom. The desks, the walls and floors, the classroom itself appeared to have been well used. My cousin, Johnny, and I sat in a desk on the first row on the far left side of the room opposite a large sandbox on a high table. The sandbox contained a few toys and what probably passed as arts and crafts projects. We were not allowed to play in the sandbox; it stood as a permanent first grade exhibit. Nursery school and kindergarten did not exist at our parochial school.

The desks showed signs of much wear and abuse. Deep gouges in the dark oak desktop bore the crude initials of former occupants. Ink stains near the recessed inkwell showed unsuccessful attempts to refill pens. Ballpoint pens probably did not exist then and would not have been approved later. The dark brown bare wooden floors were mopped at the end of every day and oiled with a pungent wood preservative at least every fortnight. Between the intense traffic of sixty little pairs of feet and the constant invasion of dust from the outside playground the floors took quite a beating.

The bare, grassless ground, often dotted with mud puddles, within the quadrangular structure of the school and convent became our playground at recess. I don't remember any playground equipment like swings and monkey bars being there. Instead, we had organized play led by Sister Mechtilda's assistant, an attractive 4th grade girl named Betty. Betty led us in games like Red Rover, Loop de Loop, and games of catch with a large, melon-sized rubber ball. The ball was so worn that there was not a trace of paint or design left on its soft, dull, pink surface that was almost sensuous to the touch. Betty would stand in the middle of a wide circle and start passing the ball around. If someone dropped the ball, Betty picked it up, returned it to the next child in the circle, and we continued to pass it around. The ball was Betty's province. It, like the sandbox, was off limits to us.

A narrow walkway led from an inner corner of the school opposite the first grade classroom to a small vine-covered grotto in front of the convent and school and just inside the walled entrance at the street. The grotto, an ivy-covered shrine to the Blessed Virgin Mary, contained a statue of Our Lady. She stood facing out from the enclave, her arms outstretched as though to greet worshipers. A lovely garden surrounded the shrine all year long, but in spring the school conducted a special service each day during the month of May. Each school day morning the four elementary grades proceeded in double-filed ranks to the grotto. The little girls showered rose petals along the path leading up to the grotto. The boys walked solemnly by their sides. We all sang a special hymn devoted to Mary as we proceeded: "O Mary we crown thee with blossoms today, queen of the roses, queen of the May..." After the whole school assembled at the grotto we recited a litany to the saints and paid homage to Mary through song and prayer. It was a beautiful ceremony that I will always cherish and remember.

Memories of grades two through four at St. John elementary school are less vivid but I still remember our teachers: Sister Cyril, 2nd grade, Sister Cabrini, 3rd grade, and Sister Placidus, 4th grade. The second and fourth grade classrooms were on the opposite side of the quadrangle, the third grade classroom on the upstairs level, the only one not located on the first floor of the building. Sister Cabrini was a lively little nun who was also a dancer. She taught us dance steps for the school recital. We danced to "School Days" for the Christmas show. Classmates Jaynell Froisy and Toby Orillion were the lead dancers in our class and also the most popular. From the dance routine we learned rhythm, coordination, discipline, and teamwork. It was an enriching learning experience not soon forgotten. I still know the dance steps!

***

Prayer punctuated schooldays in the morning before class, at noon before lunch, then again in the afternoon before classes resumed. These rituals structured the day and at regular intervals signaled what was to follow. We recited the prayers by rote and I didn't pay much attention to their content. "Amongst women," from the phrase "Blessed art thou *amongst women*," in the Hail Mary sounded like "a monk swimmin'." I pictured a slimy goggle-eyed creature thrashing about in a muddy pond. But I did pray and firmly believed in God. *Who made you? God made me. Why did God make you? God made me to know, love, and serve Him in this world and to be happy with Him forever in the next.* We studied these questions and answers in the *Baltimore Catechism* from the primary grades through high school. Each year's edition carried the same basic questions, but the answers got longer and more complicated. Catechism was always taught during the first period of every school day.

I made my first confession and First Communion when I was seven years old. I learned about mortal and venial sins and therefore about guilt. I learned that I had a soul that was depicted in our catechisms as an empty milk bottle, with little dark splotches for venial sins and a totally black bottle for mortal sin. Since we were not yet taught about sins of the flesh, the only mortal sin I could conceivably be guilty of was murder. But there was no one I hated enough to kill and would not have had the nerve or the strength to do that anyway. Despair was also a very serious sin but I had a hard time getting a handle on that one. To give up hope I guessed was pretty serious. But why do that, I thought, when there was so much to live for? No, I didn't think I had to worry about despair, either. But I could more than qualify for venial sins and pepper that milk bottle with black dots: sassing and disobeying my mother, teasing my sister and brother, not doing my chores at home, being late for school, not doing or completing a homework assignment, acting silly and disruptive in class. As soon as I learned the words, cursing and taking the name of the Lord in vain frequented my vocabulary.

So when it was time to make my first confession I had a bunch of sins to disclose. I just hoped I would remember them all. I also worried about the penance the priest would give me. How many Our Fathers and Hail Mary's would I have to say in atonement for my sins? Some priests were stricter than others and were known to assign heavy penances—as much as a decade from the rosary. But I came to realize in those early school years that confession was more than facing up to my sins but also an opportunity to talk to God, to ask Jesus for forgiveness and for help with the challenges in my young life. It was the start of a relationship. I knew that Jesus would always be there for me when I wanted to talk.

Having received the sacrament of Penance through confession, my sins were forgiven and I was ready to receive the Lord through Holy Communion. The consecrated host, a quarter-sized disk of dried bread contained the body of our Lord, Jesus Christ. What was it like? I wondered. How did it taste? Did I chew it up or just swallow it? I had a whole day to try to stay good before I received communion. If I committed any sins in the interim, I would have to go to confession again and I sure didn't want to do that. I imagined going into the confessional and saying: "Bless me, father, for I have sinned. It has been one day since my last confession."

That would be too embarrassing. The priest would probably say: "What? Back already?" I tried to be on my best behavior and to avoid conflicts for the rest of the day.

Finally, early in the morning, the day arrived for our First Communion. The boys wore white shirts and dark ties, the girls in white-laced dresses. We all knelt at the rail in front of the altar. When it was my turn, an altar boy held a silver bread plate called a paten under my chin to catch any pieces of the host that might break off. The priest held the host between his thumb and forefinger, offered it to me, and said "Corpus Christi," the body of Christ. I opened my mouth wide and stuck out my tongue. When I felt the host I quickly withdrew my tongue. The host was dry and tasteless. I tried to swallow it whole but my mouth was too dry from fasting—no food or drink since the night before. I had to break the host with my teeth before I could get it down. I was told that the Lord was present in even the smallest piece. I wanted Him to be safe within me.

Now first communicants, we then filed back into our pews, the girls on one side of the center aisle of the church, the boys on the other. We knelt and prayed in thanksgiving and for family, friends, and those in need. What was it like for Jesus to be down there inside of me? I wondered. He would stay with me as long as I remained in the state of grace, free from sin, we were told. I thought about the day ahead— school, my classmates, games, the fun things I normally did, all of which brought opportunities for mischief. It wasn't going to be easy.

***

In the first grade I had a crush on Gwendolyn Rodriguez, a raven-haired, blue-eyed, fair-skinned little beauty. She lived on Haase Street, just a couple of blocks away. My sister, Jean, knew of my attraction and would tease me by playing a little ditty she made up on the piano: *Gwen*-do-lyn, *Gwen*-do-lyn, *Ro-o*-dri-i-guez, she would sing and play in syncopated rhythm. I blushed and mildly complained to Mama. Actually, I liked the attention.

Gwendolyn and I and sometimes one or two classmates walked home together after school. I wanted to but didn't know how to show my attraction appropriately. I had only my parents as an example to emulate. Mama and Daddy were very affectionate, hugging and kissing unashamedly in our presence. So I thought if you liked or loved someone, it was okay to show your affection that way. No one told me that feeling should be mutual.

One day on our walk home I grabbed Gwendolyn and kissed her on the mouth. I smelled her sweetness and felt the softness of her lips. But she jerked away from me, shrieked, and ran home giggling. I guess she was just surprised, I thought.

A few days later I tried to kiss Gwendolyn again. This time she pulled away from me with such force that she fell backwards, hitting her head on the sidewalk. I tried to help her but she got up quickly and ran home crying hysterically. I was afraid that I caused her to hurt herself, but didn't know how else to express myself.

Not a one trial—or even two trial—learner, on yet another walk home, I tried to kiss Gwendolyn again. This time she held her ground. Instead of backing away from me, she pulled a thick wooden ruler from her book bag and smacked me hard across my eager face. I ran home crying from the pain in my smarting face, but mostly from shame and humiliation.

Mama, my Uncle Arthur, and Ma Ma Del were all sitting on the front porch of Ma Ma's house. "What happened?" Uncle Arthur asked. "Were you in a fight?"

Sobbing, I nodded.

"What about the other boy?" Arthur continued. "I'll bet you got him real good!"

I just nodded, too ashamed to explain what really happened.

***

In the second and third grades, all the boys had a crush on Jaynell Froisy, our little dance star. Likewise, and much to our chagrin, most of the girls were sweet on Jaynell's dance partner, Toby Orillion. The two celebrities had no competition. Gwendolyn Rodriguez had moved away, sparing me from further painful rejection and humiliation. Now I was attracted to the most popular girl. Olive-skinned, with pale-green, slanted, oriental eyes, Jaynell seemed exotic and distant.

In the fourth grade Jaynell transferred to the public Plaquemine Elementary School. Coincidentally, so did Toby. Socially, that left an even playing field among those of us remaining at St. John's. But I missed Jaynell and longed to see her. My classmate and friend, Tommy Wilbert, had a plan.

Tommy, the rich kid who sold me his old bike, like Rhodes, was an only child. And like Rhodes, he and his parents invited me for sleepovers. He was darkly handsome and clever. His dad, Tom Wilbert, unbeknownst to Mrs. Wilbert, would sometimes serve highballs to us at night. Mr. Tom also achieved notoriety—and Mrs. Zoe's wrath—by sneaking drinks to us kids at the Spedale's big western bash. Tommy lived a half mile away in a section of town called the "new addition" where, west of Railroad Avenue, Labauve Street became Labauve Avenue. Most of the newer, larger homes, like Tommy's were built in this section of town. I was impressed that Tommy's home had window air conditioners.

Tommy also liked Jaynell and figured out her schedule at Plaquemine Elementary School. She rode the bus to school at 9 a.m. and returned at 3 p.m. She lived two blocks from the bus stop and about four blocks from Tommy's house. Tommy planned for us to meet Jaynell at her bus stop when she returned from school. Since our schoolday schedule at St. John was from 8 a.m. to 2 p.m., we would have time to get ready for this rendezvous. I wasn't sure whether Tommy needed my presence for moral support or to show Jaynell our mutual admiration, but he wanted me there with him. In truth, neither us had enough nerve to approach her alone.

We biked to Tommy's house right after school and began to prepare for our meeting. "We'd better clean up," Tommy said and began washing his face and hands in his bathroom.

I followed Tommy's lead.

"It may be a good idea to comb our hair," he said. He carefully took a pocket comb, wet it, then parted and slicked back his hair.

I felt self-conscious but tried to follow his example. I remembered Daddy teasing me about seeing "better looking hair on salt meat." We must have looked like two little girls primping before a party.

I felt nervous and anxious. Clearly we had too much prep time.

"What will we do, what will we say when we meet her?" I asked. All of this preparation without a planned conclusion made no sense.

"Don't worry. We'll think of something," Tommy said with false confidence. "Besides, she'll be surprised to see us."

Finally it was time. We walked over to the stop and waited for Jaynell's bus to arrive. Not to appear too obvious, we positioned ourselves several yards away. The yellow school bus creaked to a stop and deposited its lone passenger. Jaynell looked so small. She wore a light yellow sweater and carried a book sack. She began walking toward us.

My heart was racing. I felt anxious, not knowing what to say or do.

As she approached us in the street, we said "Hi," awkwardly. Then Tommy, out of nowhere, threw a punch at me.

"What did you do that for?" I asked, more surprised than angry.

Tommy just shrugged his shoulders.

If she thought we had staged a fight for her benefit, Jaynell was unimpressed. She continued to walk purposefully past us on the street to her home. Our elaborate preparations were all for naught.

I wondered what Jaynell thought about us being there at her bus stop. Surely it was no coincidence. Did we frighten her? We were, after all, stalking her. Weren't there other less awkward and subtler ways to show our interest? We looked like two clumsy fools, topped by Tommy's stupid show of "masculinity" by taking a poke at me! And he set me up to be his foil. Jaynell looked shy and vulnerable—not at all the little dancing diva, aloof and unattainable. I felt ashamed and stupid.

But I got over it. The arrival of a new girl, Muriel Jean Gillis, in our class, helped a lot. A striking little blue-eyed blonde who wore her hair in thick braids like a crown around her head, Muriel Jean became my new fourth grade playmate. Without guile, I could approach her and be myself. After school, we'd play games in the street near her home, just a few blocks away. I liked her a lot but it was she, actually, who took the initiative. One day in class she squeezed into my single-occupancy desk with me. Our classmates immediately began to tease us. I was so embarrassed that I tried to push her out. I couldn't handle this public show of affection. The irony of this situation and my painful rejection by Gwendolyn and aborted rendezvous with Jaynell did not escape me. Sister Placidus intervened and I was rescued. But despite my shyness, I was flattered by Muriel Jean's attention. She boosted my self-esteem.

Sadly, at the end of the school year Muriel Jean announced that she and her family were moving away. First Gwendolyn, then Jaynell, and now Muriel Jean, I thought. I must be bad luck: If I liked a girl, she was sure to leave. Sister suggested that Muriel Jean share her forwarding address. Some of the girls asked for it. None of the boys did. I wanted to but was too shy to ask. I regretted that for years to come. I never saw Muriel Jean Gillis again and had no idea what had become of her. Feelings about girls were complicated, I learned, even at the age of ten.

The Piano Bench

The piano bench in front of our ancient upright piano[1] provided a seat for the pianist(s) and a reservoir of sheet music. It contained some of PaPa Kirk's sheet music to some old ragtime tunes, World War II music popularized by The Andrew Sisters and Peggy Lee and pop tunes of the late 1940s and early 1950s. Since Daddy played strictly by ear, he only bought sheet music to find the chords he was having trouble with. These were displayed as guitar symbols.

Although Daddy, Matt and Jean were great role models, my piano skills never advanced beyond first-grade lessons. I can't write the score but still remember the lyrics for two of my favorites:

Bone Sweet Bone[2]

Bone sweet bone, bone sweet bone
That's my favorite song,
Bone sweet bone, bone sweet bone,
Sing it loud and strong.

____

[1] The piano was a Mathushek upright, circa 1905, probably style 120. My brother, Matt Kirkland, who has an extraordinary memory, and my sister, Jean Kirkland, contributed to this story.

[2] From John W. Schaun's piano course (Pre A). It is still taught today!

Oscar the Octopus

Oscar the octopus lives in the deep,
Oscar the octopus swims on eight feet.

That was my repertoire as a pianist; but my sister Jean, graciously let me accompany her on the piano bench, play lively Chop Sticks, and sing along as she played the pop tunes we heard on the local radio and read from the sheet music. Perry Como's "If," Mario Lanza's "Be my Love," and Hoagy Carmichael's "Buttermilk Sky" were some of my favorites. I soon realized that the sheet music provided the structure, the DNA, of the songs I heard and an authenticity to the beautiful sounds I mimicked. Music timing, scale, and key gradually became familiar terms to me.

Jean could sight read but sometimes stumbled over tricky movements. I valiantly carried the tunes from memory. When he was home, Daddy would often come to our rescue.

Practicing at home with Jean on the piano bench was like a mini-rehearsal for school parties where I was often asked to sing. "Ask Michael to sing "If," "Ask Michael to sing "Be My Love," my classmates requested.

"Ask Michael to sing…"

Daddy was a self-taught musician. He learned first on a ukulele and then transferred the chords to the piano where he played a variety of pop tunes and old-time classics. Although he didn't read music, he followed the scales and notes on sheet music that he collected and stuffed in the piano bench. Daddy also had a strong tenor voice that stood out in church where he sang in the congregation and in the choir. He was in demand at weddings and socials.

When I was too small to attend Midnight Christmas Mass, Mama and Daddy let me sleep over at Ma Ma and Pa Pa Kirk's (Daddy's parents) who lived in a little brown house behind the fire station just across the street from the church. We may already have had our Christmas tree celebration because I was allowed to wear my brand new Mickey Mouse wristwatch. I remember listening to its ticking and watching the second hand sweep across the dial as I dozed off in my makeshift bed on a sofa in the living room. But when I was finally old enough, I joined the family for Midnight Mass where Daddy, as lead soloist in the choir sang "O Holy Night" in French. His voice had a silvery ring. I was thrilled. Mama's eyes began to mist as Matt, Jean, and I listened in awe. That was my father, I thought, leading the church choir in this special, traditional hymn. The choir followed him by singing a second verse, this time in English. It made an already special occasion all the more memorable.

Wanting to be just like my Daddy, naturally I, too, wanted to sing—just like my Daddy. I made my first debut at a school Easter play at the Plaquemine High School gymnasium that had a large stage suitable for concerts and shows. I was no more than ten years old. I don't remember much about the play except that all of its elements were built around the Easter theme. I stayed backstage until I got my cue to come from behind the curtain and sing the feature song, "Easter Parade." I sang one verse, just as I had rehearsed, and I was done. The audience applauded enthusiastically. I was surprised but did not feel self-conscious. Although there was more to the program, my song appeared to be the highlight of the show.

After the show people in the audience came and congratulated my parents and me. One person asked if I took voice lessons and whether I was going to sing professionally. Mama and Daddy beamed.

Daddy shook my hand. "Good job, Michael," he said. "Your voice was clear as a bell and your timing was just right."

I was surprised at all the attention I received. I was especially surprised and gratified by Daddy's reaction. He treated me as a little man, almost as a peer. Like him, I could sing, too. Later, I found a natural avenue for my singing at school class parties. "Ask Michael to sing," a classmate would say. I didn't need much encouragement—especially if the classmate was a little girl I admired. I had memorized all the pop tunes I heard on the radio and practiced with Jean at the piano: "If" by Perry Como, "Be My Love" by Mario Lanza, "Jezebel" and "Rose, Rose, I Love You" by

Frankie Laine were among my favorites. By mimicking the crooners and their unique phrasing, I didn't achieve a style of my own, but nonetheless got rave reviews for my fidelity to the stars.

We celebrated our class parties right in the classroom, usually at the end of a term or grading period. The agenda varied but usually combined academics and entertainment. I loved the spelling bees that pitted the boys and girls on opposite sides of the classroom. The girls usually won. Our home room teacher served as judge and, when necessary, referee. She selected the words and wrote the winning spelling on the blackboard. I don't remember if the winner(s) received awards, but a holy picture or medal would have been appropriate. We washed down cookies and cakes with soft drinks from the downstairs snack bar.

When asked to sing, my resonant voice carried to the adjacent classrooms, creating such a stir that I was asked to sing encores for each class. I enjoyed the attention.

Altar Boys

I spent my middle school years at St. John's, a half block up Church Street and cater-cornered from the old St. Basil's Academy where the primary grades were taught. The school and St. John the Evangelist church were collocated on the same grounds facing Maine Street. The two seemed inseparable. So much of our activities involved regular intercourse between them. Our "middle school" was simply an extension of the primary grades in elementary school. Grades 5 through 8 occupied the second floor of a red brick school building; the high school, grades 9 through 12, met on the top, third floor; and the assembly hall in the first floor or building basement was used for school functions, choir and band concerts, and dance recitals.

The church, a magnificent structure built in 1927 in Italian Romanesque style, seemed out of place in our simple little town. It had many dimensions: an impressive façade, with Doric columns, a steeple with a tall bell tower, three large formal entrances, with side doors at the front and back of the church. Inside a classic nave, with large, polished wooden pews on either side led to a marble communion rail that fronted an Italian Balestrino altar. High ceilings revealed massive beams that supported the terra cotta tiled roof. Above and beyond the altar, a choir loft cast shadows from the flickering candles below.

I became an altar boy during those middle elementary school years. The Mass was said in Latin and I first had to learn all the responses, including the Confiteor. Although we weren't required to know the English translations, daily missals were available that provided complete text for every day in each liturgical year. I got my first missal when I was confirmed. I loved the rituals of the Mass. I found them mysterious and took them seriously. I wanted to do everything right.

Fasting meant no food or drink after midnight before receiving Holy Communion the next day. When it was my turn to serve the 6 a.m. Mass, Mama would wake me at 5:30. That allowed just enough time to dress and walk to church and enter the altar boys' section of the sacristy. There from a long, open coat rack, I selected and slipped into a black cassock and white surplus. Then I went about my duties lighting the altar candles with long tapers, placing the bells and prayer card on the second altar step on the Epistle side, setting up the water and wine cruets, finger bowl and towel on the credence table to the right of the altar, and placing the closed Missal on the right, Epistle corner of the altar with the ribbons to the left. Then I met father on his side of the sacristy where he was donning his vestments. At precisely 6 o'clock I rang a little hand bell and preceded father out of the sacristy and onto the altar. There we bowed, genuflected, and father removed and handed me his berretta, which I placed on the Priest's bench far to the right of the altar. The Mass had begun.

At 6 a.m. Low Mass only one altar boy was needed but typically I had a partner to share the altar duties, where there was much bowing forward and toward each other during our responses. Novices like me sometimes mumbled the responses if we didn't have them completely memorized, hoping that father wouldn't notice. He usually did, however, and would call us on it after Mass.

"You're supposed to have memorized the responses," he would say. "Read from the prayer card if necessary, but don't give me a lot of mumbo jumbo."

Ringing the bells at specific instances could also get out of hand. Our altar bell was like a miniature xylophone and quite resonant. We rang it at the Offertory, the Sanctus, the Consecration, and at Holy Communion. We had to be alert to the beginning of each specific part of the Mass as the bell's sequence signaled the start. Right or wrong, it was always best to ring the bell on time, whether or not the sequence of tones was correct.

As an altar boy I also assisted the priest as he dispensed Holy Communion to the communicants. I held the paten under the chins of the people kneeling at the altar rail as father reached down in the ciborium he carried and with a thumb and forefinger deftly lifted a host and placed it gently on each outstretched tongue while invoking "Corpus Christi," the body of Christ. I became familiar with the regular congregants at the 6 a.m. Mass that included all twelve of the nuns who taught us at school. And I began to recognize the variety of each of their tongues: fat and wide, slim and pointy, pale and crusty, pink and smooth. Their appearance seemed to match the affect and personality of their owners. With their eyes closed and eyelids fluttering, they eagerly awaited the reception of Our Lord. I felt privileged to participate in such a personal and spiritual ceremony. Afterwards the lay parishioners crossed themselves and went back to their pews. The nuns, as a group, filed back to their front row pew. Father and I then returned to the altar where he took the paten from me and with a cloth brushed any host crumbs into his chalice.

An alcove off to the right of the altar had kneelers where worshippers could follow the Mass up close. Two of my big brother Matt's classmates, Billy Williamson and Roosevelt Kirkland, frequently heard Mass there. When I served, they would try to get my attention by lip-syncing the word "wine" while simulating drinking. They wanted me to save any leftover wine for them after Mass. I knew it was wrong, the wine being consecrated into the blood of Christ, but wondered what they would do to me if I didn't comply. Usually there was no wine left over anyway, the priest having emptied the chalice as he washed down any remaining crumbs from the host. Otherwise I would have had to confront the big boys waiting for me in the sacristy.

At some High Masses, funerals, and benedictions, the altar boy had to prepare a censer with incense and swing it back and forth from a long chain. The motion fanned the incense and kept it burning and smoking. When I first started serving, I asked the older boys how many times was I supposed to swing the censer back and forth?

"Till you get tired," one of them laughed.

But the object was to keep the censer going until father took it and tilted it in the direction of the Blessed Sacrament in the Tabernacle at the center of the altar.

Before Sunday High Mass, an altar boy rang the church bell in the steeple from a long rope that hung down in the baptismal font area in the front of the church, opposite and to the left of the first rows of pews. At five minutes before the hour, the altar boy pulled the rope to start the sequence. The bell itself was so heavy that it took the entire weight of a small boy, like my friend, Marvin, or me, to pull it down. But when the bell swung back up, it would actually pull us off the floor as we clung to the rope. Marvin took special glee in this ritual as I watched him rise up from the floor, his freshly shined brown shoes dangling in the air.

The church bell was also rung solemnly to announce the approach of a funeral cortege as it left the Wilbert Funeral Home and crept up Church Street for services. An altar boy climbed up a ladder on a wall inside the balcony in front of the church and entered the belfry of the bell tower through a trap door. There inside the belfry chamber a lone bell hung, massive and imposing. Because of the risk involved in climbing up to the belfry, and the heft and dexterity in handling the bell ringer, an older, bigger altar boy was charged with this duty. As soon as the lead hearse was spotted on Church Street, the altar boy rang the bell once every 30 seconds until the cortege proceeded up the street and assembled at the church. The altar boy lifted the heavy ringer to the inner side of the bell and let it fall to the other side. The bell responded with a resounding *dong*.

There was a surprising amount of space in the belfry chamber—enough for one boy and an assistant. Sometimes I accompanied Matt and Farrell for this ritual. They probably felt that my presence was an encumbrance, but I told them "How else can I learn?" in justification.

The view from the belfry of the tower was magnificent. Not only could one easily spot the funeral cortege, one also had a birds-eye view of the town, the locks, and the river. There was nothing else like it. On our own, and without permission, Marvin and I frequently climbed the forbidden ladder up to the belfry to take a clandestine peek at our town. We loved secret clubs and hiding places. The church belfry was the ultimate refuge. Who could find us there?

One moonlit night on the way home after a Boy Scout meeting, my friends and fellow altar boys Billy Wilbert, Lou Brown, my cousin Johnny Carville and I were crossing the churchyard when we saw what appeared to be movement in the bell tower.

"Look," said Billy. "Something's moving in the steeple."

We all looked up at once and the shrouded head of a woman within the belfry of the tower seemed to turn slowly from one side to the other. We stopped dead in our tracks.

"You're right, Billy," Lou said, "but what could it be?"

"It looks like the Blessed Virgin Mary," Johnny said.

"Naw," said Lou. "It's just a shadow."

"Maybe," I said, "but a shadow that moves."

We stood and waited a few minutes in the cool night air. Then the figure reappeared and moved from right to left in the bell tower.

"Oh my God," Billy said. "There she is again."

The figure now seemed more distinct and deliberate in its movement, almost as though to give us a better look.

"It really does look like Our Lady," I said.

"Yep, more than anything else," Lou admitted.

"Maybe she's trying to talk to us, to give us a message," Johnny said.

"Then let's show some respect," Billy said. " Kneel down and listen."

We all knelt down in the churchyard, still dotted with half-sunken brickbats left from the church construction over twenty years earlier. We watched in awe as the figure continued its movement in the bell tower.

"If we pray to her, maybe she'll talk to us, give us a sign," I said.

As if on cue we all began to recite the Hail Mary. "Hail Mary, full of grace, the Lord is with thee," we began as the figure continued its procession in full view of us all. Passersby in cars may have wondered what four boys were doing kneeling down in the churchyard but no one stopped to ask. We said a decade of Hail Marys.

Then the sky darkened and the bell tower was no longer illuminated. The figure was gone.

"Do you think she heard us?' Lou asked.

"She hears all of our prayers, "Johnny said.

We stood up and began to leave the churchyard.

"Let's ask Father Barbier about it," Billy said. "Meanwhile, we should keep this whole thing to ourselves."

We agreed to secrecy and went home, thrilled that we had been witnesses to a visitation. There were known miracles of the appearance of Our Lady at Lourdes and Fatima. Why not here at St. John the Evangelist church in Plaquemine, Louisiana? But why had she chosen us to make her appearance?

Father Barbier, our Associate Pastor, was a practical, learned man who had studied for the priesthood in France. He spoke French, English, and, of course, Latin fluently. He was our school bandleader, parish choir director, and had composed music himself. He hunted, liked sports and occasionally joined us in an informal game of catch.

We met father in the sacristy the next day and shared our story. He was impressed that we believed we had witnessed a visitation.

"Boys, I don't doubt for a minute that you believed what you saw was real," he said. "And I'm impressed by your faith. But let's consider the conditions. There was a full moon last night with a few clouds drifting in the sky. A full moon casts shadows—in this case, in the belfry that looked like the profile of a woman's head. When the clouds pass by the moon the shadows appear to move, too. So your figure seemed to move from right to left."

"As the clouds passed by the face of the moon, Father?" Billy asked.

"Right," said Father. "And then another cloud would do the same thing. What you witnessed was several clouds passing in front of the moon in succession. At the same time, the moon changes its position in the sky during the night."

"Do you think we were being silly?" Billy asked, feeling somewhat admonished.

"Not at all," said Father. "Often, as we know, God speaks to us in strange ways, even though in this case there was a physical explanation."

"Can we still keep it a secret, Father?" Johnny asked.

"Of course," said Father. "Your secret's good with me just as if you had shared it in confession."

"And our prayers?" I asked. "Do you think Mary still heard our prayers, Father?"

"Of course," Father reassured us. "And keep praying to her—and for me, too." He smiled.

"Father Barbier is smart!" Billy declared as we left the church.

"Yeah," said Lou, "and we ain't."

Even so, why did the shadow look like the Blessed Virgin Mary?

***

Throughout most of my middle school years, my duties as an altar boy ran the gamut of Low and High Masses, funeral Requiem Masses, benedictions, weddings, Forty Hours Devotion, and Lenten services including the Way of the Cross. Then between the seventh and eighth grades a new assistant pastor joined our parish church and with his arrival brought a whole new approach to altar boy service.

Father Caillouet was a tall, imposing man with strong opinions. As assistant pastor, he had no formal responsibilities and wanted to make his mark by doing something new and different. He was big on formality and looked for ways to distinguish the altar boys beyond their routine duties. He wanted to establish an elitist group of altar boys in an organization called the St. John Berchman's

Sanctuary Society. It was like a little club or fraternity. Composed of students, the society required organization and leadership. Officers were elected and I was made president. We met weekly and I followed through on various agenda items, including ordering our very own St. John Berchman's Sanctuary Society Manuals that detailed our duties and responsibilities over and above those we had learned as altar boys.

I accepted the responsibilities of my new office without enthusiasm. Somehow the pure and simple duties of an altar boy were subsumed by this new and bureaucratic organization. My God, we were a *Society*. Fr. Caillouet, on the other hand, was very much the advocate of pomp and ceremony. To me, there was plenty enough ritual in the Latin rite of the Catholic Church. As a pre-adolescent, I was more rebel than conformist. I had an innate resistance to authority. In class, I was often disruptive and enjoyed the attention I got. I'm not sure but think that the rebellious element of my leadership got me elected president of the Society. If Michael did it, my friends would, too. If I rebelled, so would they.

Either by coincidence or to force the issue, several of us altar boys planned to skip school on the very day we were to have our weekly Society meeting. We left school at noon, crossed the bridge over Bayou Plaquemine, and began hitchhiking on the highway. We caught a ride on a flatbed truck headed north for Port Allen, ten miles away. We huddled together, with nothing to hold on to but the splintery wood surface of the flatbed, as the truck barreled down the highway at 60 mph. We were thrilled—the ride adding to the excitement of our illicit adventure. At Port Allen, we crossed the river on a ferryboat to Baton Rouge and went to see a movie at the Paramount Theater. The movie, *The Thief*, a cinema noir starring a sultry Rita Gam and Ray Milland, was dark and mysterious with little dialogue. I doubt if the *Catholic Action*, the church paper that approved or condemned movies, sanctioned it.

The next day was a day of reckoning at home and at school. I also had to face Fr. Caillouet. He was furious—his anger seemed to inflame his nostrils and magnify his pale gray eyes that flashed at me. He seemed more upset that I missed our meeting and had, in fact, led what amounted to an insurrection, than the fact that I had skipped school. He began to grill me.

"Where were you yesterday?"

"Baton Rouge, Father."

"After School?"

"No, in the afternoon, Father."

"Didn't you know we had a meeting?"

"Yes, Father."

"And you went anyway."

"Yes, Father."

"What did you do on your holiday in Baton Rouge?" He smirked.

"We saw a movie, Father."

"What was the movie?"

"The Thief." I felt that this admission was tantamount to confessing to a mortal sin. A deep blush crept up my neck to the side of my face.

Fr. Caillouet looked at me with contempt. He then began a recitation of my responsibilities, how much I had disappointed him and the Society by failing to fulfill them. He promised to expect more of me by way of compensation and that he would make sure I followed through.

"What do you have to say for yourself?" My accuser asked.

"I'm sorry I skipped school and missed our meeting, Father."

"Didn't you realize it was wrong?"

"Yes, Father, I'm sorry I did it because I know it was wrong." I felt that I was making a public confession of a sin normally confined to the privacy of the confessional.

Mama, of course, was very disappointed in me and embarrassed by not being able to explain my whereabouts when the nuns called to report me missing. Her punishment didn't hurt nearly as much as the knowledge that I had disappointed her. I thought a lot about the whole incident and felt that, given the circumstances, I no longer wanted to be an altar boy. I knew I wouldn't be able to do a good job because my heart was no longer in it.

The next day I turned in my resignation and my St. John Berchman's Sanctuary Society Manual to Fr. Caillouet.

I never served Mass again.

My fellow truants claimed that they "quit when Michael quit."

The Shotgun House-Part IV

The Show

We had two movie theaters in town when I was growing up. Theater Wilbert, originally an opera house built in 1918, was later converted into a movie theater showing first silent, and then talking films. Mama, I was told, operated a player piano to accompany the drama acted out in the silent films. She also first met Daddy at the ticket booth of the theater. He was so smitten that he became a frequent moviegoer there. Thus began a lifetime romance from which all of our family sprang.

My great Uncle Lionel Delacroix—PaPa Del's brother—managed Theater Wilbert. He also built and owned the Osage Theater on Court Street. I remember going there before it burned down in 1943. I especially remember the rich smell of popcorn billowing out of the machine next to the refreshment bar. Sparks from the machine may have ignited a fire on the carpeting. No one knew for sure. Remarkably, within two years Uncle Lionel rebuilt Osage Theater and opened for business to an eager audience.

We didn't go to movies, we went to "The Show," short for picture show. At first Mama would take me, and then, when I was a little older, I'd go with Matt and Jean. When I was too little to go to the men's room by myself, Mama would take me to the ladies' room, which was like a luxurious lounge with cushioned chairs and sofas, mirrored walls and adequate privacy. My earliest moviegoing memories are of Theater Wilbert's ornate balconies with brass rails, muraled walls and ceilings depicting dancing ladies in colorful costumes. I saw there an early, animated black-and-white version of Gulliver's Travels where the sleeping Gulliver was pinned down by a swarm of frantic Lilliputians. Later I was introduced there to horror movies and terrified by Boris Karloff's "Frankenstein" and Bela Lugusi's "Dracula."

I was drawn irresistibly to horror and loved to be scared. One movie particularly struck me: "A Walk with a Zombie." Set in the West Indies, the movie involved a woman in a coma who sleepwalked to the voodoo drums in a neighboring village. Something about this pale, gaunt but beautiful woman rising from her screened, canopied bed, descending the stairs of a palatial home deep in the jungle, and walking through cane fields to the rhythmic drumbeats both fascinated and terrified me. When I first saw this movie with Mama, I was so scared she had to take me home. About a year later the movie was re-run at the theater and Matt and Jean planned to go.

"Mama, can't I go, too?" I asked.

"No, Michael," Mama said, "you were so scared when you saw this movie the last time, I had to take you home."

"But I'm older now, Mama, and it won't bother me. Please can I go?"

Matt and Jean looked at me skeptically. I could see Mama softening. She wanted me to go if I could enjoy myself and knew I'd be disconsolate if forced to stay at home. Finally, after much back and forth, she relented.

The experience of going to the show was very much a part of my growing up. Part of the ritual was getting one of my favorite treats—a bag of popcorn, a Milky Way candy bar, or a package of Charms hard candy. Then I was all set.

But soon the mood of the movie began to engulf me. The voodoo drums and the sleeping woman who looked dead to me, rising from her bed, leaving her house and gliding through the fields had me on the edge of my seat. I began to howl.

"C'mon, Michael," Matt said. "You said you wouldn't be scared."

"But I can't watch anymore," I cried.

Minutes later in the theater lobby, Jean called Mama on the house phone. "Come get Michael," she said. "He's scared!"

"Not again!" Mama declared. "I should have known."

Not wanting to interrupt too much of Matt and Jean's enjoyment of the movie, Mama walked to the theater to rescue me.

I never heard the last of this story.

First with Mama, then with Matt and Jean, and later by myself, I enjoyed my little commute to the Osage Theater. My Uncle Lionel named the theater after a grove of Osage orange trees that populated a large tract of undeveloped land at the western edge of town that he and PaPa Del owned. Leaving home, I would cross Railroad Avenue and follow a rail spur that paralleled Haase Street, where my cousins, the Simpsons, lived. Often, I would pick up little Deas to join me on our trip to the show, just a few blocks away on Court Street.

As relatives of Uncle Lionel, we had free admission to the show. But the family insisted that we pay at least the tax—two cents for children under twelve and six cents for teens and adults. The movie bill changed three times a week, with the main feature on Sunday, Monday, and Tuesday, a B or cinema noir movie on Wednesday and Thursday, and a western with a serial on Friday and Saturday. With our low-ticket fare, I often saw three movies a week without straining my allowance. A typical moviegoing week might include "The Unconquered" with Gary Cooper, "The Beast with Five Fingers," starring Peter Lorre, and "Riders of the Purple

Sage," with Roy Rogers and Gabby Hayes. The Saturday feature movie was followed by a cartoon and a serial that we called the "...continued." The very first such serial and my favorite was "The Crimson Ghost." The worst possible punishment Mama could impose on my bad behavior was to forbid me to see a Saturday movie. Then I wouldn't know what happened next in the "continued" and would have to get the information second hand. This didn't happen often but when it did, I was just miserable.

Moviegoers accessed the new theater via two entrances: the main entrance, for whites, at the front on Court Street and a side or back entrance for coloreds. A dual, back-to-back screen faced a white audience to the front and a colored audience to the back. The programs were identical. The Osage Theater was the first example of a "separate but equal" public facility in town, which made Uncle Lionel somewhat of a progressive for the times. But I was to learn that separate entrances did not denote equality.

The show was not only a good place for friends to meet, it was also ideal for early courtship rendezvous. Sitting next to a girl was a big deal. Right away word spread that you liked her and therefore she was your girlfriend. If you were so bold as to hold her hand, then you were known to be "going steady." Some older kids found dark corners of the theater for smooching. But I was still at the "puppy love" stage of my pre-puberty youth, limited to supervised kissing games like "spin-the-bottle" and "post office."

Summertime

Summers centered on swimming and baseball. The city pool and the ballfield were all within walking distance of the shotgun house. The pool was open from 7 a.m. to 9 p.m.; the ballfield was available during daylight hours. Typically, I swam in the morning from 7 to 9, played the first baseball game of a double header from 9:30 to noon, the second game from 1 to 3 p.m., swam from 3:30 to 5:30, then again in the evening from 6:30 to 8:30. I was in the water so much my swim trunks never dried out all summer long. The only thing that slowed me down was an occasional summer cold or an earache from too much swimming under water. By the end of the summer I looked like a brown twig.

A dark green building, the swimming pool bathhouse sat across Haase Street from the town power grid we called the power house. As we approached the pool, we heard a low hum from the electrical equipment at the power house. This noise let us know we were getting close. I always associated the pool with that sound. Some of the neighborhood boys organized a sandlot baseball team called the "Power House Panthers." The water in the pool was almost as dark green as the bathhouse building that surrounded it. It was loaded with chlorine so dense you couldn't see more than a foot below the surface. This made it especially challenging when you tried to capture someone under water during a game of tag.

Although Matt and Jean could swim well before I learned, Mama actually was my coach. She would sometimes hold me in the shallow, three-foot end of the pool while I practiced my strokes. Then, when I seemed to be making progress, she would release me and let me flail away at the water as I tried to swim to her on my own. She was patient and encouraging. I felt safe with her. As I gained confidence, with her guidance, I was able to swim a few yards by myself. Each time she greeted me with a hug and words of praise. We kept up this routine, gradually extending the distance between us. When I could swim across the pool without her assistance, Mama declared that I was a swimmer. I was 7 years old. After that she would feel confident for me to go swimming with Matt and Jean, while she took care of things at home. But I remember her spending a lot of time with us in the pool—even the afternoon and evening swims. Daddy, who was at work, rarely joined us.

"Ready to go swimming, doodler?" Jean would ask early in the morning as she stood at the foot of my bed, already dressed in her bathing suit.

"OK," I'd say sleepily.

"Maybe we can break the ice," she said. The first one in the pool was credited with "breaking the ice." To do that you had to queue up at the pool entrance well before opening time at 7 a.m. We were never quite that early. Word passed quickly each day as to who the eager swimmer was. Dressed to swim, he only had to drop a towel in the dressing room, take a quick shower and jump into the pool. The deep 8-foot end of the pool was closest to the dressing room. That person then became the celebrity of the day at the pool.

When we weren't swimming, we were playing ball. We didn't have organized baseball teams but chose up sides simply by designating captains who alternately made selections until we had a quorum. Rarely did we have a full nine-man squad. As a result, outfielders and infielders had a lot of ground to cover. I liked to play outfield and second base. I was a good fielder and had a strong arm, but was a spotty hitter.

We converted the football field at Plaquemine High School into a baseball diamond. The stadium bleachers were at the far side of the field, our makeshift diamond on the opposite side. Balls hit over the fence or into the bleachers were automatic home runs. Only the bigger, older boys achieved this. A straightaway center field hitter, I never could pull the ball well enough to clear the fences.

Sick at home

I played hard and wore scabs on my knees until I graduated to long pants. Mama often said that I was accident-prone. I was not a sickly child but I had my share of childhood maladies: mumps, measles, chicken pox, whooping cough, diarrhea, infections, colds, flu, and broken bones. There was no better place to hunker down during those times than the shotgun house. Mama indulged me with hot soups, cream of wheat, poached or soft-boiled eggs—food that was easily digestible without upsetting the stomach. Ice cream was a favorite for sore throats.

Doctors made house calls back then. I can faintly remember Dr. Barker, our family physician, checking on me when I had the chicken pox. My eyes were so swollen I could barely see him. Dr. Barker had a warm, friendly manner that always made me feel better after a visit.

Mama also helped me heal and cheered me up. Before running an errand, she would ask: "Michael, what can I get you from the store?" "A Batman comic book," I would answer. The caped crusader, my favorite superhero, never failed to boost my spirits. I would avidly follow his crime-fighting missions with Robin, his ward and chum. I liked to pretend that I was Robin and that Batman depended on me. We made a good team.

In two separate incidents, I broke an arm and a leg while playing football. The first happened when I was about ten. A neighbor, Gregory Landry, an older boy Jean's age, tackled me in the side yard. I fell hard on my right hand while trying to break the fall. An X-ray, a cast at the Plaquemine

Sanitarium, and a couple of days rest got me back to playing again, but no football for a while. I had a clean fracture of the wrist.

The second incident took place in the lot behind the sanitarium. We played baseball and football there. I was twelve. This time in a game of touch football, Billy Wilbert, Tommy's cousin, sidestepped me and I lost my balance. In an effort to break my fall, I put all of my weight on my right leg. A sharp, excruciating pain shot up through my leg and I collapsed on the ground. I didn't think I had broken anything at the time. But since we were so close to the hospital, one of the boys in the group got an attendant to roll out a wheelchair and push me back to the hospital. The X-ray revealed that I had fractured my shinbone (tibia). It was not a compound fracture but a hairline vertical break within the bone. To stabilize the entire leg, the hospital installed a damp, smelly cast from my foot to my hip. When the cast dried, they provided a pair of crutches for me help me walk.

I felt pretty weak when I got home and probably looked pale. Mama and Daddy thought that a shot of whiskey might help to revive me. That was the only time I was allowed any alcohol. The first night was the hardest during my recovery. I could feel tingling within the cast and wanted to scratch my leg in the worst way. I had to wait a full month before the hospital cut the cast right above the knee. Immediately I felt lighter and free to move around.

Recovery from my broken leg took much longer than my broken arm and therefore more time convalescing at home. My classmates brought me fruit, get-well cards, and my homework assignments from school. Billy visited often, feeling guilty because he thought he had caused my injury. Daddy had a squirrel hunting dog named Jack—a dark gray and silver long-haired dog similar to but smaller than a shepherd. On a nice day Jack would keep me company on the front porch as I rested with my broken leg propped on a chair. I don't remember if Daddy was successful hunting with Jack. Eventually he found another home for the dog with a family in the country who had adequate space. Although I missed Jack, I accepted Daddy's decision; he didn't want Jack to experience the same fate as my first dog, Prince, who picked up a disease from his wanderings and died on the front porch.

I remember the semi-sweet smell of ether in the Plaquemine Sanitarium. It was pervasive: up and down the wide corridors, in the patient rooms, even in the front lobby. I don't know why this anesthetic was so loosely controlled. I only received it once when I was admitted to the hospital for a tonsillectomy. Then, while the doctor and staff made small talk, I fell into a deep sleep, only to be greeted by smiles and cheerful banter when I woke up, seemingly moments later. A frosty glass of coke with a straw was my reward. I hardly noticed the smell of ether then, but on subsequent visits to the hospital it was omnipresent. At home I was treated to lots of ice cream to aid in my recovery.

Boy Scouts

Besides Daddy, one other man really stood out in my life as a role model. J.E. Dupont, a World War II Marine veteran and P.O.W., led our local Boy Scout Troop 21. Short and stocky with close-cropped dark brown hair, J.E. had a faraway look in his eyes that seemed not to focus. Malnutrition from his Japanese captors made him visually impaired. He could recognize people and objects accurately but needed a large, thick magnifying glass for reading. When he looked at you, his gaze seemed to be off to the side. Mentally sharp, logical, with a gentle, low-key attitude, he seemed to bear no other scars from the war.

Our troop met each Monday night in the basement of the Knights of Columbus, K.C. Hall on Main Street, less than two blocks from the church. J.E. taught us to stand at attention, to salute, and to align ourselves in ranks. When we "dressed right," he told us that if done correctly, all we should see would be the nose of the boy at the very end of the file. We always teased that boy for having such a prominent nose that we could focus on. J.E. was firm but gentle and never raised his voice or lost control. When a boy got unruly, J.E. made him run through a belt line where the other boys formed two parallel columns and lashed the bad boy as he ran. Sometimes several of us were made to run this gauntlet. We never questioned the justice of J. E.'s punishment; it always seemed appropriate for the infraction.

On some nights after our meeting, J. E. would take us over to the churchyard where he would officiate a tackle football game. Despite the fact that we were playing without protective gear—helmets and pads—and that the churchyard was still dotted with half-sunken brickbats from construction over 20 years earlier, no one got hurt—at least not badly.

J.E. also led us on hikes and overnight camping trips where we learned to cook over open campfires. Frozen ocean perch, thawed and cooked in a pan, was one of our favorite entrees. For himself, J.E. ate simply—canned sardines and crackers. After supper, we sat around the campfire while J.E. regaled us with stories of the war and his imprisonment by the Japanese.

"What was the battlefield like, J.E?" Lou asked. The flames from the campfire reflected the anxiety in his face.

"You have no idea," J.E. said. "Body parts strewn all over—arms, legs, heads..."

"Did you get any?" Lou hoped J.E. would share more of his actual combat experience.

J.E. didn't respond but stared vacantly at the fire.

"Can you tell us about being a prisoner?" Billy asked.

J.E. seemed more attentive. "What would you like to know? I can tell you P.O.W. camp was not like Camp Istrouma."

We laughed nervously at his comparison with our Boy Scout camp.

"They were very strict and you were punished for the slightest infraction. You got no second chances."

"Like what?" Billy insisted. J.E. whet our appetites for more details.

"I'll give you an example. Rations were tightly controlled. One prisoner tried to smuggle an extra carton of cocoa in the empty canteen holder on his web belt."

"No seconds, right" Marvin quipped. "So they found out?"

J.E. nodded. "A guard brushed against the prisoner and noticed something shaking in his 'empty' canteen holder."

"So they beat the crap out of him, right?" Marvin said.

"No. They executed him."

"Naw," Lou said in disbelief. We were shocked. The warmth from our campfire could not offset the chill in my bones.

"How?" I asked. "Did they let you see?" Like the child who couldn't resist seeing horror movies, I wanted to know more.

"They made all the prisoners watch as they beheaded the man."

"They cut off his head?" Johnny asked in disbelief. "What was that like?"

"Like a torrent of blood from a water spigot opened full."

J.E's stories were graphic and colorful but he told them dispassionately as though he was reading from a book or a movie script. Never emotional, there was no apparent pain or bitterness in the telling.

After his "bedtime story," J.E. said goodnight and left for his tent. Rather than go back to our tents in the dark, my friends and I huddled in our bedrolls around the campfire until it burned down to a soft glow. We remained there until the first light of dawn.

Under J. E's leadership, I quickly advanced in rank from Tenderfoot to Second Class, to First Class, and, finally to Life Scout. While I was recovering from my broken leg, several of my peers moved ahead of me in their quest for merit badges. Once the cast was removed and I regained my mobility, I began to catch up. First Aid, Swimming, Sewing, Forestry, Music, and Cooking were some of the merit badges I earned. Daddy was my counselor who approved my Forestry merit badge. Father Barbier approved my Music merit badge—although he qualified his approval by saying: "You don't know all of your notes, but deserve credit for enthusiasm." J.E., himself, monitored Johnny, Marvin and me for the Cooking merit badge. To qualify we had to make an earthen Dutch oven in Marvin's backyard. I remember

J.E's first taste test of our biscuits did not pass muster, but after we made some frenzied readjustments, he approved—and finished eating the biscuit.

At our next Honors Council meeting, I was awarded thirteen merit badges, something of a record. The event was reported in our local newspaper, *The Iberville South*. I went on to earn a total of eighteen merit badges in the Scouts, just three shy of the requisite twenty-one to qualify for Eagle Scout. But as I approached my teens my interests turned to other things.

Playing the man

Daddy's work as a lumberman took him outdoors a lot where he also indulged his love of hunting and fishing. Often after a successful hunt he would bring the game home. Squirrels, doves, quail, an occasional rabbit would be stacked in heaps on the kitchen counter by the sink. I watched in fascination as Daddy defeathered and skinned the quarry in preparation for the skillet. Mama hated game but was always a good sport about cooking and storing it. On one such occasion Daddy also brought home hamburgers for little Deas and me to eat while he and Mama prepared the game. He told us they were bear burgers made from a bear he killed on the hunt. The bear, obviously too big to bring home, was dressed at our local City Café where the burgers were made. We were in such awe that we swallowed the story whole. Little Deas' eyes were as big as saucers. *Imagine: bear burgers!*

For most of my first fourteen years I was too young to join Daddy on his hunts but I emulated him as much as I could at home. With my BB gun and slingshot, I became a young savage in the neighborhood. Daddy lectured me about safety but wasn't around to supervise me during the day. My guess is that he felt I couldn't get into too much trouble with my air rifle and slingshot. But as I continued to improve, I became more aware of the limited range of my weapons. My Daisy Red Ryder carbine and handmade slingshot could only shoot so far. The Benjamin pump single-shot air rifle became the weapon of choice among my peers. Its power extended both the range and accuracy of the shooter. After some lobbying I got one for Christmas when I was about twelve years old.

No bird was safe within my eyesight in the neighborhood. I was deadly. The poor robins that wintered in mild Louisiana were my main prey. One year I shot 60 of them—the same number of home runs Babe Ruth hit in a single season—a milestone that did not escape me. But I was not a wanton killer. The robins were like game to me and I cleaned and froze them in the refrigerator. Mama, always the good sport, cooked them for me at lunchtime. I ate every one of them.

Less lethal, my slingshot gave the birds more of a sporting chance. Again, I had Daddy's tales of his boyhood prowess to emulate, like hitting a dove on the wing with a biblical sling, the kind David used to kill Goliath. But when I was fooling around with my conventional slingshot on the front porch late one afternoon, Ingrid, Mr. Fryoux's granddaughter, began to tease me. Ingrid was a little pest whom I found annoying. My guess is that she was about seven or eight years old. She probably had a crush on me and teased to get my attention. To scare her away, I shot a rock from my slingshot towards the flower trellis near where she stood on her front porch. She immediately started screaming and crying. The rock had apparently ricocheted off the trellis and struck Ingrid near the corner of her eye. Both households erupted.

Daddy ran over to the Fryouxs to check on the little girl. When he came back he was furious. By then I had retreated to the hallway. "What were you doing?" he yelled.

"I wasn't trying to hit her," I tried to explain.

"Don't you know you could have put that kid's eye out!"

Then I felt an avalanche of blows to my head and body as Daddy pounded me. When I collapsed on the floor, he kicked me.

"Michael," he said, "I've told you and told you about being careful but you just won't listen."

I don't remember when he stopped hitting me but I was able to crawl to my bed in the back room where I began to cry.

But Daddy wasn't finished. He found my Benjamin pump and went to the back yard and proceeded to slam the barrel of the gun against the top edge of the cast iron side of the barbeque pit. The impact of each blow vibrated through the air and I felt that he was still trying to punish me. Clearly, his rage was not sated. It was not the force of his violence but his enormous restraint that impressed me. He could have crushed me like a fly.

Later, probably after a conversation with Mama, he came to my bedside where I was still crying. He asked how I was feeling.

"I'm OK," I sobbed, still feeling sore all over.

"I'm sorry if I hurt you," he said. "I guess I went too far."

"I'll be OK," I repeated.

"You sure can take it.

" But, Michael, you know how I've always warned you about being careful with your guns and slingshots. You know how I've always preached safety to you."

"I know. I'm very sorry. I promise to be careful from now on." Mostly I was sorry that I had let Daddy down, and that my careless behavior had almost caused a serious accident. More than anything I wanted to please my Daddy and for him to be proud of me. What hurt the most was the feeling that I had failed him.

According to her mother, Ingrid's hysterics were mostly from hurt feelings. My gun, of course, was destroyed, the barrel broken clean in half. It was never replaced.

First Love

At about the time I reached puberty at age twelve, I was attracted to an older, more physically mature classmate, Betty Bourgeois. Betty had thick, dark brown hair that framed a full and sensuous face with bright blue eyes that were warm and friendly. Her body too was full and rounded like a mature young woman. A mutual attraction started innocently enough but soon we were known to like each other. She was my girl and my peers knew and more or less respected it. Upper classmen were downright envious.

We didn't date exactly but arranged to meet at the show. On our first meeting there we sat next to each other midway down an unoccupied row off the right, side aisle. When I reached for her hand, she took mine in hers and pulled it across her breast. I had never touched a girl there before and got excited. Betty just smiled at me invitingly. As I leaned toward her I pressed my lips against hers. She smiled at me, inviting me back for more. I was aroused and breathless. Clearly, she liked what we were doing. We kept up this routine throughout the movie, totally ignoring what was on the screen. As often as we could, we continued to meet this way.

One day on a hunting trip behind the levee, Tommy Wilbert asked: "Is Betty your girl?"

"Yes," I was proud to declare.

"But she's fourteen and you're only twelve."

"Yes, but we like each other." I was confident that was all that mattered and Betty felt the same way. Tommy, I sensed, was a little jealous.

Outside of school and the show, Betty and I spent a lot of time on the phone with each other. There I learned that she was the youngest child in a large family. When she was just a little girl, her mother died from smoke inhalation during a house fire. Except for her sister Carolyn, her other siblings lived away with families of their own. I felt privileged that she confided in me about her family and life without her mother.

Betty's phone was on a party line, however, making private telephone conversations awkward. Even when I got a busy signal, I could sometimes hear muffled sounds in the background. Once when I was trying to get through, I heard the faint sounds of a trumpet. Tommy played the trumpet in the school band and I suspected he was trying to serenade Betty with his virtuosity. Betty was probably more amused than impressed.

Betty lived in the country down Bayou Plaquemine at the Enterprise Plantation where her father was overseer. One Saturday morning Tommy and I rode our bikes down the dusty gravel road that led to her home. Betty, wearing a light blue blouse and tan shorts, greeted each of us on the front porch with a glass of water. She looked so fresh and pretty in those shorts. Tommy more or less behaved himself and didn't try to stage a little fight as he did two years earlier with our aborted rendezvous with Jaynell.

That spring at a class picnic down the bayou, one of the boys started a movement for Betty and me to kiss. "We want to see Michael kiss Betty," that boy said. "Yeah, c'mon Michael and Betty, let's see you do it," a girl chimed in. Neither Betty nor I wanted to make a public display of our affection. But our friends—boys and girls—ganged up on us, some holding Betty on the ground, while others pushed me over and on top of her. In that position—and with so much "encouragement"—Betty smiled up at me and I kissed her. "Yay!" our audience responded with a round of applause.

The tension broken, we resumed our other picnic games and activities. But some of the girls in our class didn't like the kissing demonstration and began to badmouth Betty. "She likes the attention," one of them said. "Such a flirt," said another. "Well it's not like it was her idea," said a third in Betty's defense.

Betty and I then decided to escape the picnic for the time being to a nearby café. Betty found a honky-tonk tune on the jukebox there called "Nobody's Business" and kept playing it over cokes during our break.

One night, Betty slept over at a girlfriend's home in town and invited me over. The parents were away at the time. Betty and I kissed and petted with abandon. She led me out into the backyard where we held her each other and kissed in the moonlight. I had never felt the warmth and softness of her body before. She coaxed me along and I enthusiastically followed. She also let me know when it was time to stop and for me to go.

I continued to spend a lot of time on the phone with Betty. She liked romance novels and shared some of the racy parts with me. I also heard about her dates with older boys, especially a sixteen-year-old truck-driving boy she met in Port Allen.

"I met him at the rec center," Betty said. "My sister dropped me off there earlier in the day. The kids were playing some of my favorite songs and dancing. When they played 'I Wanna Be Loved', he asked me to dance. I knew the lyrics and sang along with the Andrews Sisters 'I wanna be loved…'. And he said: 'I'll love you.' I just froze. I didn't know what to do. But thank God my sister came back to pick me up. I was so relieved."

Had I been dancing with Betty I might have said the same thing. Didn't she know that? Didn't she know how I felt about her? Then why was she sharing this information with me? Because she trusted me and wanted me to know that she had a social life outside of our relationship?

I sensed she was slipping away. Still, I felt that she and I liked each other and that was what mattered. That summer, while Betty was visiting her sister again in Port Allen, I decided to find out what was going on. I hitched a ride and found Betty at the Port Allen public swimming pool.

Unlike the one in Plaquemine, the larger Port Allen pool had crystal clear light blue filtered water and three diving boards at the ten-foot deep end. I met Betty at the four-foot shallow end. She wore a one-piece blue bathing suit that hugged the contours of her body. A solid white bathing cap framed her smiling face. She seemed to be having a good time. I ignored the splashing and yelling of the kids around us. She sat on the edge of the pool as I approached her.

"Hey, Betty."

"Hello, Michael."

Something had changed.

"Are you still my girl?"

"I don't know." No longer playful, her expression was sober, her eyes clear and thoughtful.

I knew right away that it was all over between us. Betty let me down as gently as she could. There was nothing else to say. I dove into the pool and swam underwater as long as my lungs would support me. When I exploded through the surface with a gasp, Betty was gone.

At home later that day I felt sick, nauseous, couldn't eat and couldn't stop crying, mostly from my bed in the back room, where I had felt comfort and security. Returning there to lick my emotional wounds seemed like the natural thing to do. Mama didn't know what to do with me. Nothing was wrong—other than my complaining—that she could see. The worse part was that I couldn't share my grief with anyone: I felt humiliated and ashamed. But I missed Betty and loved her more than ever. I didn't realize that I was suffering from a broken heart. My first.

The Shotgun House-Part V

The Youth Center

While the new St. John the Evangelist church was being built in the early 1920s, a temporary wooden frame building was erected to house the congregation. It sat cater-cornered from the church near the Locks and across Main Street from City Hall. A large, barn-like structure, it seated several hundred parishioners. After the new church was built, this temporary structure remained for years and became an all-purpose meeting hall for church and school fairs, fund-raising pancake dinners, bingo nights, proms, awards ceremonies, wedding receptions, dances and concerts, and many other social events. But everyone referred to it as The Youth Center. Always in need of a fresh coat of whitewash, the building even served as a dance hall for our annual "Hobo Carnival."

About the time I was 13 years old in 1951, the Hobo Carnival was inaugurated to mimic the famous Mardi Gras event in New Orleans held at the same time where each year the latest King Rex was crowned. Ours was like a poor man's version of this main event. Each year *The Iberville South* posted hints about the new king's identity weeks in advance of the inauguration. Nobody guessed who the mystery king really was; only the carnival organizers knew.

I'll never forget our first Hobo Carnival. A big crowd waited in anticipation for the arrival of our hobo king. No red carpet, but a center aisle was roped off to allow his majesty to promenade up to the dais at the back of the hall. The master of ceremonies tapped on his microphone to quiet the crowd. There was still a buzz in the room. "Ladies and gentlemen," he said. "Please welcome Plaquemine's king of the Hobo Carnival."

All eyes were on the front door when in walked a little man dressed in rags from head to toe. He wore a mask and top hat that reminded me of pictures I had seen of a chimney sweep. He moved swiftly, gesturing and waving to the crowd with a brisk, officious manner. The crowd cheered and applauded not so much the king but the very idea of the carnival itself. When he reached the dais the master of ceremonies greeted him, shook his hand, turned and announced: "Ladies and gentlemen, I present to you Plaquemine's very first Hobo King!" With that, he removed the king's hat and mask, revealing a spry little man with a slate gray flattop: George Viguet, our local convenience store merchant.

The crowd went wild. "George! George!" they shouted. He shouted back at people he recognized, pointing and gesturing almost as if he was trying to sell something. Indeed, he succeeded in selling the crowd on himself, our local junk dealer and our first and most famous Hobo King.

The next year, Doc Spedale became our second Hobo King but his "talking hands" almost gave away his identity during the ceremony. Overall the carnival was just a grand occasion to let go, where young and old, rich and poor, could meet and celebrate. If Plaquemine had a spirit, it was best revealed at our annual Hobo Carnival.

There was a dance at The Youth Center every Saturday night. Sometimes a local group of young musicians played for us. On special occasions, professionals like the Dave Bartholomew band, provided the music. We were thrilled. Dave was writing music with Fats Domino back then during the early days of Rock and Roll. But mostly we danced to records, a rich selection played on a fine turntable with good amplification.

When I was a teenager, my social life entered a new phase. Not only my classmates, but also girls from other grades at St. John and Plaquemine High attended the dance and friends from neighboring towns like White Castle, Donaldsonville, and Port Allen also came. I liked to slow dance and jitterbug and found it a great release for teenage tensions. I also felt free to choose a dance partner without *liking* her. But I enjoyed holding my partner close and feeling her respond. If she liked the way I held her, she would smile, inviting me to ask her to dance again. And so it went. The Saturday night dance at The Youth Center then became as much a social institution in my life as my Saturday afternoon ritual at the show.

First Job

I got my first job working as a cleaning and delivery boy at Wilbert's dry goods store. Herd Trabeau, a family friend and one of Daddy's hunting buddies, managed the store, which featured women's clothing and shoes. The store sat at the corner of Eden and Plaquemine streets, right next to Wilbert's hardware store where I got BBs for my air rifles, pocketknives, and miscellaneous parts like screws, nuts, and washers. Other than trips with Mama, I had no occasion to shop at the dry goods store.

My duties were simple. I reported to work right after school. I first emptied all the trashcans that were placed near the end of the aisles into a huge green bin in a parking lot behind the store. Then I sprinkled a sweeping compound on the floors to keep the dust down and swept the floors with a long-handled, wide-brush broom. I swept the whole store from front to back and collected the dirt with a dustpan, which I emptied into a large trashcan that I dumped in the bin outside.

Although Mr. Herd hired me, another older man, Bill Emdy, frequently gave me ad hoc assignments. Mr. Emdy was a stoop-shouldered, gray-haired man who wore thick lensed glasses. He worked for Wilbert's both as office manager and store superintendent. He navigated in the back hall that connected both the hardware and dry goods stores. An open office with a teller window served customers with store accounts.

"Boy," as he called me or "Kirkland," (never Mike or Michael) "I have an errand for you to run." Typically, he had a package to deliver to a customer a few blocks away. I liked being responsible and getting an assignment outside of cleaning up. But every now and then he would give me a personal task.

"Boy, take this watch to Dechary's Jewelers and ask them to clean it for me." Dechary's was a prominent business just two blocks away on Railroad Avenue. I was flattered that he trusted me with this transaction and felt that it was no imposition.

One day I had an after-school conflict and asked my brother, Matt, if he would sub for me. Matt, who already had a full-time paper route, was willing to help. But I first asked Mr. Herd if it would be all right.

"Oh, so you boys want to alternate," he said in his friendly, soft-spoken manner.

I wasn't sure but guessed he meant taking turns. Matt and I then began working alternate shifts after school throughout the week and on Saturdays.

He paid us around 50 cents an hour. At the end of the week, I earned between five and ten dollars. I was thrilled to be making my own money.

Mama had a special bank account called a Christmas Club. I was impressed that she saved money in that account expressly for Christmas, her favorite holiday. Not only was that bank account a secure place to save money for a special occasion, but also, thanks to the bank, the money would grow with interest, a mathematical factor that intrigued me. As soon as I was able, I went to the Iberville Savings and Loan bank on Main Street near the church and opened an account of my own. Each week when I made a deposit I watched the balance grow.

Matt and I managed this schedule well for several months throughout the school year. One Saturday, between shifts, Mr. Herd asked to talk to us.

"Boys," he said, "the company wants to make a change and we're going to have to let you go." His eyes were sad as he forced a weak smile.

Matt and I looked at each other in surprise.

"Why?" I asked. "What did we do?"

"You did nothing wrong," Mr. Herd said. "You've both worked well here and we liked having you. The company just decided it would be more economical to have a full-time boy do the work." He seemed uncomfortable with this explanation.

I was crushed. I loved my job and the independence I felt by earning my own money.

The full-time boy, we learned, was a colored boy who didn't have a school schedule or extra-curricula to manage.

"What did he mean by 'economical'?" I asked Matt on the way home. Like "alternate," the term was not yet a regular part of my vocabulary.

"That the Wilberts were probably paying the new boy less per hour than they were paying us while getting a full day's work out of him."

"But that's not fair. They could still have hired the colored boy to work days while you and I could continue working evenings and Saturdays."

Matt shook his head at me impatiently. "Don't you see? They want to get more work for less money. They're not interested in being fair."

Matt was always so logical, a trait I admired but often found frustrating.

As for the black kid who displaced us, we didn't know his circumstances but figured that he needed the job to help his family. His hiring had nothing to do with equality. It was just business.

Measuring Up

By the time I was thirteen, the incident with Ingrid and the slingshot well behind me, I got a reprieve. Daddy bought a 20-gauge Remington pump action shotgun for Matt and me to share. Finally, I had the opportunity to actually enter Daddy's world as his hunting companion. I would no longer need to play the man with my BB guns and slingshots. At first, he took Matt and me out separately to practice shooting and to get the feel of the gun. Though lighter than a 16- or 12-gauge shotgun, we found that the new 20-gauge gun, with the modified choke it provided on its 30-inch barrel, gave us a range and spread that was ideal for bird hunting. But my real baptism with my new gun was my first duck hunt.

The Thanksgiving holiday weekend in that year brought abnormally cold wet weather to south Louisiana. We headed to Daddy's duck camp deep in the swamps near a bayou called Big Alabama. Daddy steered from the stern of our skiff while I sat in the bow looking ahead. The small, outboard motor puttered softly. I had no idea how close we were to our camp where we would start the hunt. The narrow slough was almost encased by moss-covered, low-hanging trees. Through the canopy we saw a small flock of ducks fly over us and drop down one hundred yards ahead.

Daddy cut the motor and began to paddle. "Be quiet, Michael," he said softly. "If we're lucky we may get a shot at those ducks in the water."

"Are they mallards?" I whispered.

"Wood ducks," Daddy whispered back. Normally soft-spoken, he didn't need to whisper. "Smaller and faster than mallards."

And harder to hit, I thought. My gun was loaded and I double-checked to make sure the safety was off.

*While dove hunting with Daddy and some of his friends earlier in the fall, I failed to keep the safety **on** while loading my gun and a shell went off. At least I remembered to point the gun down and away from everyone. But I was very embarrassed, even though no one said anything. I was surprised—and gratified—that Daddy didn't make a big deal out of it. Later I learned that the men asked not to hunt with me again.*

As we rounded a bend in the slough, the ducks appeared in the open water, clucking noisily, searching for food. I raised my gun.

"Not yet, Michael," Daddy said. "I'll tell you when we're close enough." We were still at least fifty yards away. He continued to paddle steadily.

Finally, when we were in range, Daddy said: "Aim at the one farthest away from the others. Take your time and when he is within your sights, squeeze the trigger."

Shaking with anxiety I pushed the stock of my gun firmly against my shoulder, lined up the bead at the end of the gun barrel with the center of the duck's profile and squeezed the trigger.

The explosion shook me and the boat rocked back and forth. The ducks took off in flight, leaving one thrashing about in the water. "I got him, I got him!" I yelled. I bagged a duck on my first shot.

"Settle down," Daddy smiled. "You'll turn us over. You could have gotten another shot or two at the ones who took off." Then, as an afterthought, "I should have alerted you."

But I was overjoyed. As I collected my prey—the dead duck—Daddy said: "I wanted you to get your first chance this way. But we really shouldn't shoot them on the water. For the rest of the hunt, we'll shoot only at ducks in flight—then we'll see what kind of a wing shot you are." He smiled at me.

I smiled back at him, buoyed by my initial success. I wasn't sure but felt that I was up to the challenge.

We continued our journey through the swamps until we reached the duck camp, a rough-hewn one room house with several bunk beds. We unloaded our gear and walked to the site where the sloughs crisscrossed and the ducks were known to roost. It was late afternoon and long shadows fell across the swamp. Birds were flying in every direction. The trees and foliage of the woods provided natural cover, obviating the need for a duck blind. Daddy positioned me on a bank about twenty-five yards downstream from his stand.

"Try to keep your eyes lowered and your head down," he said, "until they're in range. I'm going to try to call them in."

Daddy's duck caller was a small, dark, woodwind instrument about the size of a large whistle or an ocarina. He could make it sound just like a mallard hen's feeding call. Four short "quacks" on his little horn, followed by four short "quacks" again, then lots of chortling. Within minutes ducks came flying in as if in answer to a dinner call.

"Here they come," Daddy said. "Get ready."

Small groups of ducks flew across the woods and down the slough toward Daddy and me. I aimed and shot, pumped another shell into the chamber, aimed and shot again. I didn't so much as raise a feather. Although he deferred to me, Daddy was able to drop many of the ducks I missed.

"Something must be wrong with this gun," I complained. "I get a bird right within my sights and nothing happens."

Daddy came over to my stand. "Let me take a look," he said gently. He was using a Browning 16-gauge "sweet sixteen" automatic and had already bagged half the daily limit. He took my gun, aimed at the first duck that flew over, and dropped it effortlessly. "Seems OK to me," he said. "You might be shooting too fast. You got to move the barrel of your gun ahead of the duck and move with him before you pull the trigger. I tell myself to 'get on him, get ahead of him, pull,' following through with the arc of my gun all the while."

It sounded easy, and to watch him, it looked easy! But I was too anxious. By the end of the day I had expended more than a box of no. 6, 20-gauge shells with nothing to show for it. Then I realized why Daddy let me shoot that first duck on the water.

Like fishing, the best time to hunt ducks is early morning and late afternoon. Those are the times when the birds come in to feed. Early the next morning, after a light breakfast and strong coffee, Daddy and I revisited the network of sloughs where I used up a box of 20-gauge shells the night before. Other than a few chattering squirrels scampering up and down the oak trees, all was quiet, not a duck in sight.

"There's no guarantee they'll come back to the same place," Daddy said.

"Maybe we're too early," I said, still sleepy from Daddy's ungodly early morning wake up call.

"Not a chance," Daddy laughed. "They may just want a little variety and a different restaurant." He checked the horizon where the glow from the early morning sun filtered through the mist, illuminating the stumps and cypress knees in the swamp. "Well, if they won't come to us, we'll have to go to them—let's take a walk." He looked at my sleepy face and smiled. "You could probably use the exercise."

I tried to look brave. Indeed, I needed to move. I felt that I was frozen in place. "I'm ready when you are."

Daddy paused to light up his Kaywoodie pipe, that he filled with Granger *Rough-cut* tobacco. The pipe was ubiquitous on hunting and fishing trips. When not smoking, he kept it handy in his top left shirt or jacket pocket. When it rained, he could turn over the bowl of the pipe and keep smoking without losing its contents. And he could fill and light up the pipe while driving. The pipe was very much a part of Daddy's persona. A thin blue cloud of smoke formed a halo above him.

There was no discernible path for us to follow—only a trail blazed by loggers or other hunters. Using an axe or a knife, they had sliced a chunk of bark from the trees at eye level or higher from left to right at regular intervals. Daddy was familiar with these routes, having made many of them himself. We followed one such trail for a while until we came upon another slough, visible through the dense foliage. High above us and completely out of range, a flight of about a dozen mallards circled.

"Let's see if we can coax them down," Daddy said. He took out his duck-caller and began "talking" to them.

The flock banked, circled again, and began a deliberate descent. Two of the ducks broke off from the left of the flock and began to fly in our direction. Daddy kept up his frenzied call, followed by a busy chortle. The birds, looking for a hen in the water, had all but dropped their landing gear, when they would glide with their wings stationary and their yellow feet straight out.

"Wait till they're in range," Daddy whispered.

He didn't have to say anything else. I picked out a green-headed mallard drake coming toward us, set my sights, followed his path through the bare, thin trees and pulled. The bird crumpled in flight and fell on the bank just a few yards away.

"Good shot, boy!" Daddy shouted, forgetting our code of silence. "You got him before I could get a shot." Daddy was tracking the duck, too, this time not waiting for me to shoot first. He was more surprised than me.

At last I could shoot a bird on the wing. Close to frostbite, my toes tingled, but I felt warm with the satisfaction of accomplishment.

With Daddy still calling them in, the ducks seemed to be pulled towards us as though on a string. I bagged another duck. I seemed to have gotten the hang of it. I was in control.

Then, just as quickly, the birds stopped flying. Daddy realized that he was wasting his breath with the duck-caller. "Time to take another walk down the old 'Chisholm trail,'" he said. He pulled a pocket compass from his jacket and began to take a reading.

"Why do we need that?" I asked.

"As a back up," he said. "Sometimes these trails look quite different when you do them in reverse. We'll be getting farther away from the camp and our boat. If we take a back azimuth from the direction we're heading in now, we can be sure to find our way back."

This was a lesson in orienteering I had not yet learned in the Boy Scouts.

We hiked deeper into the woods. A big, stout man, well over 200 pounds, Daddy moved gracefully as he ducked beneath low-hanging branches, always making sure they didn't snap back into my face as I followed him. He bobbed and weaved like a boxer, clearly superior to the obstacles in his path. He skipped across logs in sloughs as nimble as a dancer. Here I was finally able to observe him in his element, totally engaged in his environment. Having me along didn't compromise his activities in the slightest.

Finally, we came upon another slough, more thickly encased by low hanging trees and underbrush. Daddy positioned me near a tree. "This may be a good place for them to land," he said. "Keep your head and eyes down and just wait." He walked off from me until he was out of sight and began to call again.

I heard a ruckus on the other side of the bank but refused to raise my head to satisfy my curiosity. I didn't hear Daddy calling anymore. A few minutes later he came up to my stand.

"Michael, this place is teeming with squirrels," he said excitedly. "Didn't you see them?"

"No, I didn't want to raise my head and open my eyes."

Daddy chuckled. "OK, you did the right thing, but squirrels are in season, too, and you can shoot them when the ducks aren't around."

I accepted the invitation and soon added a gray fox squirrel to my quarry.

We continued to trek through the woods, now in the late morning, the sun hidden behind low-hanging clouds sodden with moisture. A light, freezing rain began to fall—perfect weather for ducks. We came upon another slough, wider than the rest, with a high bank. There we took our stand. Daddy felt there was no reason for us to hunt from separate stands. He also could see that I was cold and wet and thought it best for us to stay together.

"I'll bet right now you'd like to be home drinking a nice big cup of your mama's hot chocolate," he said.

I nodded in agreement while raising my frozen feet up and down. Sure, I missed the warmth and comfort of home but wouldn't have traded this time with my Daddy for anything.

Just then we heard the loud shriek--*peeeww, peeeww*--of a lone Blue-winged Teal flying upstream toward us. In seconds the bird was parallel to us. Daddy instinctively threw his "sweet sixteen" to his shoulder, tracked the bird as it passed us, pulled and shot. The bird stopped instantly in a cloud of feathers, its momentum carrying it several yards farther upstream, before it descended gently into the water.

"Wasn't that a good shot, boy?" Daddy said softly.

My ears still rang from his shot and the smell of burnt gunpowder permeated the cold damp air.

I nodded in humble admiration. The best of the day, I thought.

On the way home, we had a postmortem. Daddy said: "You shot three ducks and a squirrel and got lots of action. Remember this hunt. You may not see another like it."

He was right. I never did see another hunt like that one. And I never forgot it.

The Last Christmas

In 1951, Mama and Daddy finally were able to build their own dream house. It was on a parcel of land owned by the Delacroixs and divided among Pa Pa and Ma Ma Del and four of their children: Uncle Homer, Aunt Pamilla, Aunt Carrie, and Aunt Regina (Mama). A thick grove of Osage orange trees grew there, primarily on Aunt Carrie's lot. Three of the lots faced east, side by side, on Marshall Street with Mama's on one corner and Aunt Pamilla's on the other. One of my cousins called our neighborhood "the aunt hill."

Mama chose a model three-bedroom house from a *Better Homes and Garden* magazine. It had a red brick front, white shutters, a side screened porch, and a two-car garage—a perfect layout for a corner lot. Daddy hired the Guinchards, builders from Paincourtville, to build our house. Not your typical development builder, the Guinchards were quite creative and often suggested options, like the wall-to-wall two-person desk at the window in the boys' room. Daddy handpicked much of the timber for the foundation pilings (Guinchard would not build on a concrete slab), the gum wall paneling and the hardwood flooring. He could tell you the type and grade of wood in each room and was quite proud of it.

All that summer and fall in 1951 we watched each phase of the construction and by the Christmas holidays the house looked complete. But because of the time-consuming inside work yet to be done, the new house was not yet ready for occupancy. Matt, Jean and I wanted to move in by Christmas Eve and complained a lot about it. Mama, always sentimental around this time of year, reminded us that this would be our last Christmas in the shotgun house.

Before our traditional Christmas tree exchange of gifts, I decided to give Mama a surprise present just from me. Mama had lots of dishes and cookware, but was short on serving dishes, especially something to keep biscuits and dinner rolls warm while company was waiting. I found a nice dish for that purpose at The Village gift shop located on the street right behind the Osage Theater. I paid for the dish and had it gift wrapped from my Christmas Club savings account. I also threw in a box of Whitman's Sampler chocolates to "sweeten" the deal.

I presented the gift to Mama one afternoon when we were alone. I wanted to do this privately so as not to embarrass Matt and Jean in case they hadn't bought a gift for Mama, too.

"Michael, this is so thoughtful of you," Mama said as she unwrapped the gifts. "The serving dish is just what I needed."

"I wanted to do something for you for a change," I said. "You've always been so good to me." She was so appreciative I wished I had done something thoughtful like this long before.

After hugs and kisses and a few grateful tears she said: "But Michael, where did you get the money?" It had been a few months since I was fired from my job.

"Oh, I still had money in my Christmas Club savings account. That's what it was there for."

The holidays were also a time for mischievous pranks from kids who had extra time on their hands.

"BLAM!" went an explosion on the front porch, accompanied by the clattering sound of metal.

Daddy ran out to the porch and found the charred pieces of our mailbox scattered around the porch and front steps.

"What was that?" Jean asked.

"Somebody's idea of a joke," Daddy said. He wasn't smiling.

"Must have been a pretty big firecracker to do that," I said in wonderment.

"Either a cherry bomb or a two-incher," Matt declared.

"What a mess," Mama said as she observed the damage. "Now who would do a thing like that?"

"I don't know," Daddy said, "but if they come back, I'll be waiting for them."

Things settled down for the next few days. We concluded that some of Matt's or Jean's friends may have been responsible—older kids with a fast car. Busy with Christmas preparations we put the incident behind us. Then one day as we were settling in for the night another explosion shook our composure.

"BLAM!" went a firecracker on the front porch.

"Not again!" I yelled.

But Daddy wasn't caught completely by surprise. As the pranksters were driving away, he ran out of the house, jumped into his 1950 Plymouth sedan and started after them.

I was impressed by how quickly Daddy reacted.

He chased the culprits across Railroad Avenue and up Labauve for about six blocks until the getaway car disappeared in heavy fog.

"All I could see were the taillights," Daddy said later. "But at least I gave 'em a scare."

Indeed, whoever it was never came back---intimidated, we concluded by Daddy's aggressive chase. They didn't want to confront an angry "Mr. Matt."

That year we performed our ritual of singing carols around the tree on Christmas Eve. We had been doing this for as long as I could remember. But this year was special because it would be the last time we would sing carols together in the shotgun house. There was a sense of transition as each of us Kirkland children had grown older there—Matt, 17, Jean, 15, and me, 13. Yet it was not so much a feeling of what we were leaving behind, as it was the anticipation of what we expected to enjoy in the new house.

For Christmas I also got a present I'll never forget. Daddy hired a local bike mechanic to restore my old second-hand Schwinn to mint condition. Painted a bright green with yellow trim and yellow handle grips, new tires, wheels and pedals completed this masterpiece. Only the original frame survived but the bright new paint masked the old, faded red finish. All that for about $25. I was overjoyed and right away took the bike for a spin in the neighborhood. The bike seemed to glide along by itself.

This gift was all the more special because it converted what was old and second hand into something new and completely my own. It meant more to me than an expensive brand-new bike. I never needed or wanted another one.

The Move

We moved out of the shotgun house and into our new home all within a day. The beds and large furniture went first, probably on the back of a truck Daddy hired or rented. For the occasion, Daddy also brought down his company jeep that he used primarily with logging crews and on hunting trips. I helped load and unload small packages of our belongings—clothes, groceries, books, small appliances, our phonograph record collection. I sat in the back of the jeep, keeping our cargo stable, while Daddy drove us back and forth. The excitement of each trip brought us closer, I felt, to being fully ensconced in our new home less than a mile away. I fantasized about spending the night there, waking up in my new room and walking to the sparkling new linoleum-floored kitchen where freshly brewed coffee awaited me. In just a day that dream became a reality.

In the late spring of 1952, the pink azaleas had already peaked and other spring flowers—bright orange day lilies and yellow forsythia—were in bloom. I had just celebrated my fourteenth birthday and looked forward to moving up to the high school level of the St. John school building in the fall. Although the house was now complete and ready for occupancy, the land surrounding it still needed work.

We first had to clear the yard of construction debris, bricks, scrap lumber, trash—a lot of it. Daddy equipped me with a shovel, a rake, and a wheelbarrow that I used to cart the stuff out to the street for trash removal. Next, he ordered several loads of river soil dumped unceremoniously in the side yard near the driveway. There I shoveled the black, loamy soil into the wheelbarrow and dumped each load over the yard surrounding the house. I then smoothed out each load of dirt with a rake until it covered the entire weedy but grassless yard. We continued this activity before, during, and after the move in preparation for planting St. Augustine grass later that would become our lawn.

Daddy seemed to enjoy working with me and often complimented my progress. "You're a pretty good truck driver," he would say. I was thrilled that he trusted me and allowed me to work with him as a team. No skill was involved—just hard manual labor. But I felt up to the task and happy to be working with my Daddy and feeling his approval and recognition.

Now empty, the shotgun house looked deserted, almost as if no one had ever lived there. I walked through each room, furnishing in my mind how our family made its own personal stamp: the rug, sofa set, and console radio/phonograph in the living room, the maple table and piano in the dining room, the appliances and cupboard in the kitchen, the three distinctive bedrooms, especially the back room where I had spent countless hours playing. We had happy and sad moments there, living life fully as a young family. I processed these memories while still focused on the overwhelming and exciting adventure of moving to the new house.

The back yard and shed, where I created so many make-believe games, looked deserted, too. Perhaps the new renters also would have children who could make up their own imaginary characters.

Across the street, the Spedale home looked resplendent as ever, the grounds featuring Mrs. Zoe's latest landscaping project. I had spent much of my 14 years there, too, and kept the memories intact. Rhodes would be home from boarding school soon to discover our long-anticipated absence.

I got on my bike to take one last ride through the neighborhood—past Rinaudo's store, the Neubig's home, the old "haunted" house, to the foot of the levee. I climbed to the top and surveyed the area back of the levee that had been my extended backyard and wilderness playground for so many years. Then I turned around and looked west where a descending sun illuminated my path. I walked back down the levee, got on my bike and rode past my old home, the Spedales, across Eden Street past George Viguet's store, across Railroad Avenue and up the long, wide stretch of Labauve Avenue to Marshall Street, and then on to my new home.

I never looked back.

I had everything to look forward to. How could I know that I was leaving the happiest years of my life?

Mama's Photo Album

Mama collected photos of us from the time we were born until we grew up, had children of our own, then grandchildren, and beyond. Most of the photos I selected, with the help of my sister, Jean, came from Mama's album. I tried to select the ones that showed us at or near the house during the years 1938-1952. By no small coincidence, several of the photos show us at Easter. Like Christmas, Easter was a special holiday that we celebrated with new clothes to usher in the rites of spring. Since we also celebrated my birthday in May, spring became my favorite time of year.

Easter 1943. Matt, Jean, Cousin Lina Baby, Cousin Little Deas, and me, age 5. When we were small, a wagon was the perfect prop for our pictures. After the "shoot", we could all play on it.

Little Deas and me, age 5. Two "mean little hombres." My first cousin, Deas (Henry Deas Simpson III) and I played, hunted and fished throughout our childhood.

Matt, Jean, and me, age 5, in front of the house. I loved to wear boots and boot pants and strut around mimicking Mussolini, the Italian dictator during WWII.

Matt, Jean, and me, age 6. Unlike the others, this photo was taken at a studio in the Hotel Silber, next to The Mission soda fountain on Main Street. I enjoyed cherry cokes and nectar sodas at The Mission.

Matt with his pet cat (1948). He liked cats better than dogs because cats seemed more independent. Good view of the front of the house without the shrubbery.

Jean, Cousin Anne Neubig, and Mama (1949). Anne adored Jean and looked up to her as s big sister.

Me in my Boy Scout uniform, age 12. I was probably a Tenderfoot scout at the time. MaMa Del's house is in the background.

Easter with Daddy and Jean (1951). I was almost 13.

Easter, Matt and Jean (1951).

Easter, Jean and me (1952). I was almost 14.

The author on his way to "The Show" (1951). I was 13. The pretty girl is my sister, Jean.

The Spedale home (date unknown) at the corner of Labauve and Eden streets. Resplendent at the time the same way Mrs. Zoe maintained the house and grounds.

Piper

Alvin Piper worked as a foreman at the lumber mill Daddy managed for the Wilberts in Plaquemine. A light-skinned Negro with delicate features, Piper carried himself with the dignity and pride of a man accustomed to doing good work. Daddy frequently bragged on Piper. "There is nothing that man can't do. Just give him a job and he'll do it—better than anyone else." In addition to his work at the mill, Piper was often called upon to build things, employing his considerable skills in carpentry, a trade in which he particularly excelled. Piper remained in Plaquemine when Daddy moved on to manage a mill 40 miles away in Maringouin, Louisiana. But the two men stayed in touch, Daddy frequently calling on Piper to help him with projects or to seek his advice. He liked Piper very much.

One day Piper stopped by our new house to visit Daddy. I was in the yard tending to the pigeon coops my friends and I slapped together with scrap lumber that I retrieved from a loft in the garage. Not working from a plan, the available material pretty much dictated the shape of the coops that would eventually house my pigeons. Located beyond the driveway in the back corner of our lot, but next to our sparkling new house, the misshapen, dilapidated, and unpainted coops were an eyesore that somehow my parents tolerated.

"Who built those houses?" Piper asked as he got out of his truck.

"My friends and I," I said.

"What you going to keep in them—chickens, rabbits?"

"Pigeons."

Piper smiled. "Pigeons, huh, that close to the ground." The floor of one coop was less than a foot off the ground. "Your daddy help with this project?"

"No, he just gave us the wood. My friends and I wanted to build it ourselves."

"Shows." He nodded his head thoughtfully. "Did you ever use a level?"

"No," I wasn't quite sure what he meant, "but we did take measurements."

Piper then went to his truck, pulled a level from his toolbox and showed me how to determine whether an object was horizontal (level) or vertical (plumb) by observing the shape of the liquid bubble in the center of the tool.

"Your daddy's a good man," Piper continued, "and he's been good to me."

"He thinks you're a good man, too."

"There is nothing Mr. Matt won't do for you if you have a problem."

I remembered the occasions when Daddy's workers stopped by the house to ask for a loan and Daddy, listening to the man, would reach for his wallet, never asking for or expecting repayment. Piper, however, always so competent and self-sufficient, didn't seem to fit among Daddy's debtors.

"Your daddy could have built these houses for you but he wanted you to build them yourself. That's the only way you learn how to do things, you know."

Later when Piper met with Daddy, I heard them talking and laughing about the sorry state of my pigeon coops. Still, I was proud of my coops and the home they would eventually provide for my pigeons.

I didn't see Piper again until Christmas of that year (1952), the first Christmas in our new house. Piper and his two teenage sons, darker than their father and just as handsome, came to the back, kitchen door. Every visitor came to call that way, ignoring the more formal front entrance to the house. After parking in the driveway, one could walk through the garage to the porch and the kitchen door.

We had just finished breakfast, having gone to Midnight Mass the night before. Daddy and I were still in our pajamas and robes. It was a crisp, mild Christmas morning, typical for South Louisiana. Daddy ran to the door to greet our visitors.

"Well look who's here," he said. "Good morning and Merry Christmas."

"Merry Christmas, Mr. Matt," said Piper. "We just wanted to pay our respects before the day got away from us."

"Well come right in and we'll start the celebration."

In the kitchen Daddy poured each of us a whiskey, neat—the first drink of many in a long day of Christmas cheer. Then Daddy led us to the back yard where the morning sun had already brightened the day. There we raised our glasses in a "Merry Christmas" toast and shook hands all around. I felt honored that Piper and his sons chose to visit us at the start of the holiday. It all had to do with the special relationship he and Daddy had. I could see how pleased Daddy was, too.

We didn't see or hear from Piper for months after that Christmas visit. Then one day Daddy came home looking pale and somber. "I just heard that Alvin Piper died," he said.

"Oh no," said Mama. "When—how?"

"Six months ago. I don't know the circumstances. Didn't even know he was ill." Illnesses—even deaths—among colored families sometimes didn't make the local newspapers. Daddy sat down at the kitchen table and put his head in his hands.

Mama tried to comfort him. Her feelings were always near the surface—especially when it came to Daddy. "Oh Matt, I'm so sorry. I know how much you liked Piper."

"Didn't even have a chance to say goodbye or pay my respects."

"There must have been an obituary in the paper and a funeral."

"Maybe, but I knew nothing about it."

"Six months ago was around the time Piper and his sons paid us a Christmas visit." It was June now and the summer heat already oppressive.

Daddy got up then and walked out into the back yard where Piper, his sons, Daddy and I had assembled that fine Christmas morning. He didn't talk anymore but seemed to be processing all that had happened. He looked profoundly sad but there was nothing anyone could say or do to comfort him. He was the picture of utter despair.

I felt so bad for Daddy. I had never seen him this way before—even when years ago we received the news of Uncle Lionel's death. He and Piper were more than friends: they loved each other. Would it have made a difference if Piper had been white? *Of course it would.* He and Piper would have been hunting and fishing buddies, drank beer and enjoyed cookouts together, watched ballgames, socialized with family. If only Piper had been white. But who in God's name created such restrictions—that white people and colored people cannot mix? Who created this segregated society that Daddy faithfully subscribed to and ultimately was victimized by it? That, I was sure, was part of what Daddy was trying to process and agonize over as he sat alone grieving in the back yard.

Maud

Maud Dorsey, Ma Ma and Pa Pa Del's colored maid and housekeeper, was also a regular member of the household. I learned from Mama that Maud was a teenager when she came to work for Ma Ma. She and Mama, who was the same age, helped raise the younger children in the family: Uncle Homer, Aunt Carrie, Aunt Ernestine (Beanie), Aunt Pamilla, and Uncle Lionel. Maud continued to work for my grandparents and stay close to the family well after the children grew up.

My first memories of Maud come from my early years in and around the shotgun house. The back porch was the scene of a summertime ritual: eating watermelon and having your face "washed" with the clean rind. Maud, a sweet but brusque woman, with large, flat features, gave me my first initiation. After I finished eating a generous slice of watermelon, she unceremoniously took the empty rind and scrubbed it across my face. She was none too gentle and I was a little hurt that she would treat me that way. Otherwise she was always kind to me. She and Mama laughed and explained that it was all in fun as part of a long-standing tradition. My face scrubbing was like an initiation.

Typically, on one of my make-believe adventures, I would climb over the hot tin roof of the shed and down the slope to the other side. There in the fork of a large, shady camphor tree I would talk to Maud. I could barely see the outlines of her black face through the screened window above the kitchen sink. Often only the glow from a gold tooth revealed her presence. But she would talk to me and sing to me good-naturedly as I sat in the tree, regaling me with "'Possum in the 'simmon tree, raccoon on the ground.. ,'" and other favorites. She called me "Michael Henry"—why, I'm not sure because my first cousin Deas was named Henry Deas. Anyway, sometimes she would offer me a treat. "Henry," she would say. "Do you want some stale cake?" I would always answer in the affirmative. She would then laugh and say "Ha! That boy will eat anything!" I gathered that I saved her a trip to the garbage can. Maud and I had good times. She also convinced me that I could capture a bird by dropping a teaspoon of salt on its tail. Try as I might I could never get close enough to my prey to administer the paralyzing agent. I was a great source of amusement to Maud.

Maud lived in a small frame house in an undeveloped "suburb" of Plaquemine called Seymourville. Ditches instead of sidewalks lined the unpaved roads there. From her home early in the morning, Maud began her commute to Ma Ma and Pa Pa Del's house about a mile away. She always carried an umbrella, called a parasol, to protect her from the blazing summer sun and the frequent thundershowers. In the fall during the sugarcane harvest, she moonlighted by joining the laborers, male and female, in the cane fields outside of town. With her strong hands and back, I felt sure Maud was productive. I didn't know exactly when she participated in this annual ritual or whether she took time off from her job at my grandparents' house. She would simply say: "Time to go cut cane."

Often, she brought home a ripe stalk of sugarcane and shared it with us kids. With a cane knife or a large butcher knife, she sliced a section and peeled off the outer skin. The hard, unprocessed sugar fruit yielded a sweet juice unlike anything we had tasted before. Though hard to chew, the raw sugar cane was worth the effort. On our bikes, we sometimes chased down overloaded sugarcane trucks en route to the refineries. We could easily pull off some of the stalks hanging loosely from the load. We had to be careful, though, because often an apparently loose stalk of cane was actually secure and would pull the bike rider forward as the truck sped on. In the same way, but on foot, we also chased down open boxcars loaded with sugarcane as they rolled on rail spurs through town.

I knew nothing about Maud's family but occasionally she would make weekend trips to "the city," New Orleans, assumedly to visit kin. When she returned, she always had a happy glow about her. Her visits must have been rewarding.

At our new house on Marshall Street we continued being neighbors. Ma Ma and Pa Pa Del also built a little house on the opposite side of our block, across the street from Uncle Homer, next door to Aunt Pamilla, and cater-cornered from Aunt Carrie's new home. It was wonderful being surrounded practically by Mama's whole family in our new neighborhood. In addition to maintaining our own lawn, I was "hired" to cut the grass in Pa Pa Del's back yard. Sometimes, when I wasn't prompt, Pa Pa got behind his lawn mower and tried to mow the lawn himself. This stirred up both Maud and Ma Ma. "What's that old whitehead doing out there?" Maud said. "I've told Mr. Mille he should not get out in that hot sun," Ma Ma chimed in.

Embarrassed, I would run over and insist that Pa Pa let me finish the job. Afterwards, Maud treated me to a tall glass of iced soda.

Sometimes they invited me over for dinner, the noontime meal. This was the main meal of the day, typically with pork chops, mustard greens, mashed potatoes and iced tea. For dessert we had apple pie, chocolate or vanilla custard.

"We gotta keep our yard man well fed," Pa Pa said.

"Mmm hmm," Maud mumbled under her breath winking at me. "And keep you inside."

After the noontime dinner, Maud cleared and reset the table with the plates turned over for the evening supper of leftovers and light fare—a custom carried over from the plantation days.

Daddy kept his jeep at home during the summer and let me practice driving it in Aunt Carrie and Uncle Deas's vacant lot next door. They were the last to build their home and the lot was also handy for ball games and picnics. When I was reasonably proficient with the stick shift and clutch, Daddy let me take the jeep out on the open road where there was not much traffic. By the time I was 15, I was eligible to take the driver's test and get my license. I was thrilled.

I welcomed any excuse to take the jeep out on the road to run errands, almost always taking the long way to extend the trip. I volunteered to drive Maud home in the afternoon after she finished work. Maud sat next to me in the passenger seat wearing a wide smile bright enough to shine through a dark and cloudy day. I then became her regular chauffeur and she no longer called me Michael or Michael Henry but simply: Friend.

At Christmastime the Delacroix families held an informal reunion of gift-giving and socialization. Maud was there not as a servant but as a participant in the festivities. She started a tradition of "passing the hat." She would grab a hat and pass it around the group of us, demanding cheerfully that we "put something in the hat!" Invariably she would catch us by surprise as we fumbled around searching our pockets, wallets, and purses for any loose change or bills. Afterwards we seemed to feel satisfied by the generosity that we had been goaded into. Instead, we could have raised the money ourselves and presented it to her as a gift or Christmas bonus and spared her the indignity of passing the hat like a beggar. It never occurred to us to treat Maud as a member of the family, even though she had helped raise many of us and had touched the lives of all of us.

In addition to my yard work, I took Pa Pa Del to High Mass with me on Sunday mornings. I was glad to have an excuse—this time with the family car—to "run an errand." But I truly enjoyed having Pa Pa at my side for Sunday services. I took comfort from the way he held on to my arm for support.

But age and illness began to creep up on Ma Ma and Pa Pa Del. Pa Pa failed first. One of my relatives pulled me out of the show one night with the sad news that Pa Pa was in the hospital and was not expected to make it through the night. The family gathered in his room at the Plaquemine Sanitarium. His voice was weak and his breathing labored but he managed to speak to us. We all felt it was our last opportunity to say goodbye. Pa Pa died early the next morning.

The next day we assembled at the funeral home where Pa Pa lay in an open coffin with a rosary wrapped around his large hands. Looking down at him, we could appreciate his larger than life features and his thick shock of white hair. He seemed totally at peace, without pain or fear. Maud was among the last mourners to arrive at the wake. She knelt down at Pa Pa's coffin and cried painfully from the depths of her soul. Only then did I realize that despite her joking and teasing about Pa Pa, she loved him dearly as much as if he were her own father. I was moved by her grief.

Years later, after Ma Ma, too, passed away, I looked for Maud during my visits home. I checked on her to see how she was doing and left money for her as often as I could. She was still Maud to me and I was still Friend to her. I felt bad that I couldn't do more for her and didn't have the impression that my parents, aunts, and uncle were doing very much, either. But my first cousins, Janie and Linda, the youngest of Aunt Carrie's six children stayed in touch with Maud on a regular basis. Janie, aka "Big Butt" to Maud, and Linda provided essentially a "meals on wheels" service for Maud when she was ill or otherwise incapacitated. That gave me some assurance that at least the youngest of our family looked after Maud.

On one of my home visits, Mama told me to be sure to call Maud. She had been asking about me.

"Hello, Maud, how are you?"

"Hey friend, it's good to hear your voice."

"It's been a while, hasn't it? How have you been feeling?"

"Doin' all right, I guess, but the doctor say I had two heart attacks."

I was shocked. "Wow!" was all I could say.

"Wow is right! It surprised me, too."

"Well obviously you've got to try to take it easy—not do too much."

"Yeah, that's what they all say, but I'm not so good at taking it easy."

"No, but you have to." I didn't know what else to say. "So who's looking after you?"

"Oh Janie Big Butt and Linda—they come around once in a while and bring me food, sometime do some shopping for me."

"Well I'm glad to hear that."

"Yeah, I tease them a lot but they good girls and I know they love their old Maud."

"We all love you, Maud, you should know that."

"The Delacroixs, the Simpsons, the Neubigs, the Kirklands, you are all my family, too."

After my conversation with Maud, I told Daddy that she had had two heart attacks.

"Two heart attacks!" he said. Obviously, he didn't know and I guessed that Mama didn't know, either.

Six months later on my next visit I learned that Maud had died. Neither of my parents went to the funeral and I doubt that any of the family attended. Maybe Janie and Linda went. I'd like to think so. I'd like to think that some members of my family showed appreciation for her life that she shared unsparingly for us all.

But I was proud that my relationship with Maud had grown to where she regarded me simply as "Friend."

The Mill

The summer after I graduated from high school in 1956, I found myself at 18 with nothing to do until I started my freshman year at L.S.U. in Baton Rouge in the fall. Having the whole summer to loaf and indulge myself didn't bother me. After all, I received honors at graduation, including the American Legion award for scholarship. But I knew, and was sure my classmates knew, that my cousin Johnny would have easily copped all academic honors, including class valedictorian, had he not left St. John's for the priesthood after our sophomore year. I wasn't even in the running for that honor, left in the dust by the brainy girls in my class.

Anyway, Daddy wasn't hearing about my hanging around, loafing all summer.

"Can't find a job?" he asked.

"Nope".

"Did you try looking?"

"Yes, Daddy, but there's nothing out there."

"I doubt if you tried very hard." He wasn't impressed by my job search.

Daddy had worked hard all his life and had no tolerance for laziness. When my brother Matt and I tried to sleep in late on a Saturday morning, Daddy would come in from mowing the lawn or washing the car and bang on the outside door to our room. If he was up working, everybody should be up.

When Daddy finally decided to put me to work at his mill, I was ready to go, eager to do a man's work for a change. I wasn't intimidated by laboring with Daddy's full-time staff. After all, this was how he worked as a young man as he moved up the ladder into management. Now he ran a crate box factory and veneer mill for Rathborne, Hair, and Ridgway Company in Maringouin, Louisiana.

With my jeans, polo shirt, cowboy boots, and ducktail haircut, I thought I was hot shit.

"You sure don't look like a worker," Daddy said as we walked toward the entrance to the mill. He wore khakis in spring and summer and double-breasted suits in fall and winter. But, after all, he was the boss. I was a low-level laborer.

Mr. Miller, a spry, wiry little man with rimless glasses met us in front of the mill. Miller was Daddy's superintendent, the next level of management at the mill. His humorless, no-nonsense demeanor was off putting. After a brief introduction, Daddy explained that I was to start work at the mill.

"So you want me to find some easy job for him to do?" Miller asked.

"No," said Daddy. "I want you to work the hell out of him!"

Oh shit, I thought. He wants to make an example out of me, to show that the boss's son wasn't going to get any slack. Still cocky, I wanted to show I could handle anything they threw at me.

Miller escorted me inside the mill opposite the area where the softwood logs were rolled into a circular saw and planed into sheets of veneer. The veneer was stacked into bundles a yard wide and a foot deep. Each bundle weighed about 25 lbs. Miller had me working alongside an older black man with graying temples. Our job was to move and stack the bundles in an open boxcar that was parked right alongside an open sliding door to the mill. Once loaded, the boxcar would be coupled to a freight train and shipped to a customer at another mill or box factory.

Avoiding introductory formalities, Miller, indicated to the black worker that I would be helping him move and stack the veneer bundles already filling one end of the boxcar.

It seemed easy enough and if this old guy could do it, I could certainly do it—and maybe speed things up a bit. At first I was loading two bundles to every one my partner loaded. He, on the other hand, just kept up his steady pace. The bundles got heavier, it seemed, and in less than an hour I was falling behind the pace set by him. To this fellow, there was no competition but a slow and easy way to go about his job. I had made it a competition, not with him, but with myself in an overzealous effort to prove myself. I was spent. And humbled.

Miller quickly sized up the situation, told me to take a break and without criticism escorted me to another area of the mill. "There's lots more work to be done in this mill," he said.

At the far end of the mill, opposite the entrance to the box factory, we met Hamp, a foreman who supervised the processing of small wooden slats that formed the sides of the finished crate boxes. A group of black women stood on either side of a conveyor belt and as the freshly cut slats came down, they sorted and bunched them in groups of about ten high. The bunched slats were then loaded into boxes at the end of the belt and carted off on a forklift to the box factory next door.

Hamp, a blonde, stocky man with a jovial manner, introduced me to the women. "This is Mr. Kirkland's son, Michael," he said. "He's going to help you sort them slats."

The women looked at each other in bemusement and made way for me in their line. I had the feeling that no other male worker participated in this process.

"Well, I hope he don't cry," I heard one say to another.

Unlike my previous job, this one took more finesse than strength. As I tried to assemble a stack of individual slats, some of them slipped away for another sorter to pick up down the line. It took timing and coordination, skills that eluded me. But with practice, and some assistance from my co-workers, I got the hang of it.

The next day I traded in my jeans for a pair of overalls and my cowboy boots for sensible work shoes. I was embarrassed by yesterday's performance at the mill and determined to at least look and act the part of a mill worker. The women sorting slats at the conveyor belt seemed to be surprised that I came back but again made way for me in their line. Sallie, the one who had joked about me yesterday, greeted me with a big welcoming smile. Her full, parted lips, revealed two rows of bright shiny teeth. Her smooth, dark, velvety skin was immaculate. She was a full-figured young woman, compared with most of the angular white girls I dated.

Though welcome at the conveyor belt and reasonably competent with the work, I wondered if this particular job was going to be the extent of my work at the mill. I got my answer the next day when Hamp intercepted me en route to the conveyor belt. "Mike," he said, "you're doing a good job here, but I want you to try something more suitable for a young man." He led me out of the mill to a concrete strip that separated the mill from the box factory. Near the entrance, a young black man was dipping wooden cleats into a large tank of green dye.

The man, Jack, wore rubber gloves that reached up to his elbows as he dipped each cleat into the dye. Hamp explained that the cleats were dyed to distinguish the framed corners of the box from the soft, tan slats that made up the sides. I could either retrieve them from the stacks that were bundled in an open boxcar next to the concrete strip or pull one off a forklift that carried them into the box factory. This was my introduction into yet another phase of the box factory operation.

A man of medium height and build, with a tan complexion and a slight mustache, I guessed Jack was in his early twenties. He was open and friendly, with a wry sense of humor. "So you the boss's son?" His question was more a statement of fact begging confirmation.

I nodded.

"How come he got you doing this shit?" He smiled.

I smiled back. "He wants me to work here and maybe learn something."

He nodded. "Ain't nothing wrong with that so long as you willin'."

"I want to work and learn as much as I can."

"He'll like that. Your daddy sure will."

Jack and I engaged in easy conversations on topics ranging from the weather, the heat, sports, and sometimes girls. We'd take our breaks together, too. Jack had a half sandwich and I had a donut and a Coke. It felt good to have established a routine together and that I was welcome to share his.

During one of our morning breaks, Sallie, the slats sorter, walked by. Jack and I watched the rhythmic flow of her body.

"What do you think of her?" I asked.

He looked at her appreciatively. "Hips like a Jersey cow."

But there was more to my job than keeping Jack supplied with wooden cleats. The boxcar that contained them needed to be emptied onto forklifts on a regular basis. It was hot, strenuous work. Already intense outside, the mid-summer heat was stifling above the stacks of cleats in the boxcar. I joined two, sometimes three young black workers in the process of loading the bundled cleats onto the forklift. Though much heavier than the veneer I had moved on my first day, the process of moving the bundled cleats offered frequent breaks when the forklift was full. This gave us the opportunity for small talk and friendly banter.

"How old are you, Michael?" Jason, an older, black forklift driver asked.

I told him I was eighteen.

"When I was eighteen I could lift them bundles with each arm—two at a time!"

He looked strong enough now to make good on his claim but I wasn't about to respond to his challenge.

"So now you the big forklift driver," one of my fellow workers taunted.

"I did everything you're doin' and more before I moved up to this job," Jason snapped. Then he turned to me. "But, Michael, how come your daddy has you bustin' your ass out here when you could be working in that air-conditioned little office with the pretty secretary?"

This was an option that was never discussed. "He wants me to learn what hard work is all about first, I guess, like he did as a young man. And really, Jason, that's OK with me, too."

Jason smiled and shook his head. "All I can say is that if my old man ran this place, I know where I would be!"

"Yeah," chimed in a fellow worker, "there would be Jason: Chief nigger in charge!" He immediately realized he had misspoken and bent over to get a deserved kick in the ass. "Sorry, brothers."

"Watch your mouth, man," another worker said. It was bad enough to have used the N-word, let alone in front of a white boy.

I felt embarrassed for them.

Jason shook his head and backed the loaded forklift away from the boxcar. As he turned and headed for the box factory, he noticed some activity farther up on the rail spur.

"Hey, look what's going on up there," he said. In the hazy distance a crew of men armed with picks, sledgehammers, and shovels worked steadily on the rail spur.

"Who are those guys?" I asked.

"Mexicans."

"What are they doing?" asked one of my fellow workers.

"Fixing rail ties."

"Out in the open like that?" asked another.

"Ain't no other way to do it. Those Mexicans can take the heat better than most folks. That's why the railroad company hires them."

I thought of the stifling conditions in the boxcar where we worked but at least we had shelter.

From the distance we could hear a *chink! chink! chink!* as they drove spikes into the rail ties. We continued to admire the Mexican laborers, seemingly unaware of their audience.

White people, I thought, assumed that blacks could withstand the blazing sun, heat and humidity better than they. But black people readily deferred to the Mexicans for this type of work. Until then I was totally unaware of this division of labor.

By week three at the mill, I was hitting my stride. Comfortable with the work routine and accepted by my black peers, I felt satisfied by putting in a full day's work. My new crew cut felt cooler, too. But I wanted to be more independent as a worker and not have to rely on my Daddy taking me to work every day. The family car, a baby blue '52 Chevy coupe, was available, so why couldn't I commute to work by myself? The impracticality of my suggestion was obvious but this was not yet the age of car-pooling. Independence meant having and driving your own set of wheels.

Still, neither Daddy nor Mama was crazy about my making the 40-mile commute to Maringouin every weekday. Daddy came up with a compromise solution.

"How'd you like to spend the week in Maringouin?" he asked. "That would make your work week more of an adventure."

I was intrigued. "How—why?"

"You could bunk in my room behind Martin's Café."

I had forgotten about Daddy's room that he maintained for overnight hunting and fishing trips. I had stayed with him there once when I was lucky enough to join him. "Are you sure? That might be fun."

"Come on, now," Mama said. "You two aren't thinking this through. What's Michael going to do for meals? Who's going to feed him?"

Daddy smiled. "He won't starve. He can get his meals right there at the café."

"Well, there goes his paycheck."

"So what else will he have to spend that $40 on? He might as well get to know what it's like supporting himself—except for rent, of course."

"Did you ever hear of saving?" Mama was always the practical and frugal one who over the years managed the family budget on a shoestring. "And he's got college coming up right around the corner."

"Mama, other than gas and food there's nothing in Maringouin to spend my money on." That wasn't quite true. There was a bar at the café and a local movie theater in town.

On one of the first nights at my new home away from home, I tried out the bar right off the street and around the corner from Martin's Café. The bar, a hole in the wall, with a tiny table in each corner and several stools, had a thick layer of sawdust on the floor. The smell of freshly cut wood seemed to permeate my environment. Most of the patrons stood and drank right at the counter. At 18, I qualified to drink beer but not hard liquor. I came right in from an especially hard, hot day unloading wooden cleats from a stifling boxcar. I was hot, sweaty, and very thirsty. The bartender, a woman in her twenties, asked: "What can I get you, sha?" Most female bartenders greeted their patrons with this Cajun French expression for cher.

I nodded toward the dual draft taps behind the counter. "One of those."

She reached in a cooler behind the counter and pulled out a frosted mug. I watched as she carefully filled the mug from the tap, making sure the foam didn't rise more than one inch above the line of the beer filling the mug. "Try that on for size."

I didn't realize how thirsty I was. I all but absorbed the cold beer as it slipped so easily down my throat.

The bartender smiled. "My, you musta' been thirsty, hon'. Ready for another?"

A second frosted mug appeared before me. I'll savor this one, I thought. Feeling mellow now, my surroundings appeared clearer: the bar, the glasses, the bottles of liquor on the shelves behind the counter, the conversations and laughter that seemed to echo off the walls. I felt exhausted and an overwhelming drowsiness. I desperately wanted to crash in the bed in Daddy's room behind the café. I left a dollar for the two beers and a twenty-five cent tip, staggered out of the bar and on to my room where I collapsed in the bed and fell right to sleep.

I slept so soundly that when I awoke around 6:30 p.m. in the mid-summer twilight, I thought it was the next day. I was starved and quickly got dressed to catch breakfast before heading to the mill and punch the clock at 8 a.m.

The waitress at the café seemed confused when I asked for the breakfast menu. "You mean dinner, don't you?"

"No, breakfast," I insisted.

She left the menu with me and walked away shaking her head.

Sure enough there were only dinner entrées of fish and beef listed on the menu. I ordered a meatloaf and potatoes dish that I hoped would satisfy my hunger. I was pleased that hot coffee as well as iced tea was offered.

After dinner I drove to the mill. No one was there. And there were no cars in the parking lot. Daddy's office was locked up tight and the outside security light was on. What's going on? I wondered. Was I too early or was it Saturday? I was very confused. I drove back into town and noticed that as it got darker outside the streetlights came on. Finally, as I drove down Main Street, I saw a queue forming at the local movie theater. I realized then that I hadn't slept through the night and it was still the same day.

When I shared this experience with Daddy, he didn't seem to react one way or another. He didn't even seem amused. I guessed that he was preoccupied and not impressed with this latest story about his silly son. But the next day at work everyone at the mill and box factory knew about it.

"Hey Michael, we heard you came to work "early" the other night." Jason, the forklift driver, smiled. "Not much happening then, right?"

The women sorting slats at the conveyor belt were giggling. "How was your breakfast last night?" Sally asked and then convulsed with laughter.

"Now just how many beers did you have?" asked Jack as I met him at his station.

"Someone has a big mouth," I said, realizing that Daddy had shared this incident with the mill workers.

Daddy typically walked through the mill and box factory every morning at 10 and in the afternoon at 3. The image of Daddy, the boss, impressed me as he made his rounds. His thick frame and quiet demeanor commanded respect. Despite the din from the saws in the mill and clatter from the wirebound box staplers in the box factory, there was almost a hush as he walked by, sometimes greeting workers or conferring with his foremen. He projected an understated authority as the boss, The Man.

Typically, the workers took their breaks at these intervals. But nothing irritated Daddy more than to see his staff having a snack when, in his mind, they should be working. I had heard that on one such occasion Daddy chewed out Jack when he was on break. Jack never shared this incident with me.

But today, as Daddy walked by, I was angry. "Thanks a lot, big mouth," I shouted.

Daddy hesitated as if to process what I had said. He didn't answer me but kept walking.

I immediately regretted my outburst, warranted in my view, but no less disrespectful. I had no right to behave that way—especially in front of the workers. I loved Daddy and would never want to hurt him.

"Big mouth," Jack mimicked me. He was impressed that I would talk to Daddy this way. I was ashamed.

We never talked about it again.

That August I was assigned to work in the box factory.

The box factory assembled wirebound crate boxes primarily used by farmers producing Louisiana yams. Customers in neighboring states used them to ship other fruits and vegetables. The boxes were stacked and shipped in long sheets of four sections. The customer could then fold each section and secure them into boxes.

With his long overalls and soft-spoken country manner, Mr. Gowens, the factory manager, seemed more like a farmer. His staff, black and white alike, loved him. He treated everyone fairly and despite his easygoing manner ran a tight ship. Morale was high.

"You're going to like working for Mr. Gowens," Jack said. "He's a nice man."

Daddy thought Gowens was too easy on his workers. "He spoils them," Daddy said. But he couldn't argue against productivity and Gowens' numbers always impressed Daddy and his upper management.

Gowens first put me to work repairing boxes that came off the assembly line with broken slats or cleats. Sometimes the slats weren't lined up properly and just needed to be straightened. Others would split around a knot or soft spot in the wood. Still others would buckle from the stress of the stapler machine. The defective boxes were stacked next to my workbench. Armed with a claw hammer, extra staples, and good slats, I established a working rhythm. Unconsciously I switched hands from left to right as I repaired the boxes from one end to the other. One of my fellow workers pointed that out to me. Before then, I had never known that I was ambidextrous.

The stack of repaired boxes to the right of my bench began to grow. "Michael, you're making it hard for me to keep you busy," Gowens smiled. "When your stack of repaired boxes doubles the broken ones, feel free to take a break."

"Shall I take them over to the warehouse where the others are stored for shipment?" I asked.

Gowens smiled. "If you'd like to, Michael. That would be helpful."

I took a stack of five boxes and carried them out of the factory to the warehouse next door. A young black man was working there lifting boxes from a pallet the forklift driver had transported from the factory. He was stacking them high in a corner of the warehouse. "You bringing me more work?" he asked.

"I guess so," I said. "This place is all about work, isn't it?"

"Yeah, don't look like they gonna run out anytime soon. How come you hand carried those boxes over?"

"Got a little slack time fixing boxes."

"Then why didn't you just take a break?"

"Mr. Gowens said I could but I wanted to help."

He smiled and shook his head. "You must not have worked here very long—hey! You Mr. Kirkland's son?"

"Yes, I'm Michael—or Mike—take your pick." I extended my hand.

He took mine in his strong, warm hand. "I'm Wally, glad to meet you. Anyway, getting back to you volunteering for more work, I would just take it easy. Because next thing you know you'll be swamped with work."

The next day it was clear that Gowens wasn't going to keep me busy fixing boxes. "Michael," he said, "I have to ask you to help Wally stack boxes in the warehouse. I understand you met him yesterday?"

"Yes, sir."

"He needs a hand getting the warehouse inventory ready for the next shipment. Also, we don't want to get backed up here in the box factory."

"That's OK, Mr. Gowens, I'll do whatever is needed to help."

"I like your attitude, Michael, and you'll still be able to return to your repair job from time to time."

I noticed the rising stack of damaged boxes next to my workbench.

A shade darker than Jack, Wally was huskier than me, with broader shoulders and a thicker chest. He told me he practiced football with his high school team after work. I, too, had played high school football and remembered practicing in the afternoon August heat. Our coach took water discipline to the extreme, pushing our dehydrated bodies almost to the point of heat exhaustion. Sometimes we practiced into the night under the ball field floodlights. But I couldn't imagine practicing football in the heat *after* a full day's work.

We established a routine in the warehouse. Jason, the forklift driver, would drop a pallet loaded with boxes. Wally and I would lift the boxes from the pallet and stack them alongside the warehouse wall opposite the front-loading dock. When we emptied the pallet, Jason would return with another load. Sometimes Wally and I worked together on the same stack; other times we built our stacks side by side. We developed a rhythm to our work and Wally liked to sing to set the tempo.

"Fever in the morning, fever all through the night," he sang.

"Sun lights up the daytime, moon lights up the night," I chimed in.

"Hey, Mike, you know Fever?!"

"Yeah, I hear it sometimes on the radio, but I don't know all the lyrics. Who's the artist?"

"His name be Little Willie John and his song is at the top of the R&B charts."

"Must be high on the Pop charts, too." We listened to the radio a lot at home and in the car. I knew all the tunes. Frequently popular R&B and Rock n' Roll songs crossed over to the Pop charts.

As we stacked the boxes higher and higher in the warehouse, Wally continued his rendition of Fever.

Never know how much I love you, never know how much I care When you put your arms around me, I get a fever that's so hard to bear You give me fever - when you kiss me, fever when you hold me tight Fever - in the morning, fever all through the night.

"That's the first verse. You know the second?"

"Not really. You sing it all the way through and I'll try to join you the next time around."

Then Wally started singing again, the sweat dripping down his body. We were both drenched in our own sweat.

Sun lights up the daytime, moon lights up the night I light up when you call my name, and you know I'm gonna treat you right You give me fever - when you kiss me, fever when you hold me tight Fever - in the morning, fever all through the night.

We continued to work into the afternoon, finding we could keep up a steady pace that Wally had set by stacking two boxes at a time rather than trying to lift and stack several at once.

A tall shadow of a man appeared against the warehouse wall. Gowens stood behind us wearing a wide grin. "You boys keep yourselves amused by singing while you work?"

"Yes, sir," said Wally. "It helps us stay focused while making the work more tolerable."

Gowens admired the stack of boxes we lined up against the warehouse wall. "You're making good progress."

"It helps to have a partner," Wally winked at me.

I smiled. It felt good to be recognized not just by my boss but also by a fellow worker.

Just then Jason pulled up with another load of boxes on his forklift. "Hey, Mr. Gowens," he said in mock complaint. "Can you tell these boys to slow down? They're emptying each pallet of boxes faster than I can bring them more!"

Gowens smiled. "I agree, Jason," Then to Wally and me. "Take a break, boys, and try to cool off. You're already ahead of schedule for the next shipment."

We took our break over cold soft drinks in a shady spot behind the building. Wally and I talked about a lot of things. Comfortable with the conversation, I was surprised when he asked: "How do you feel about integration?"

I hesitated. I knew that Daddy, a staunch segregationist, said that it would never work. I tried to be honest. "I would probably be OK with it, but I don't think it will work."

"Too many white people against it, right?"

"Right." I thought of Daddy at the forefront of the opposition.

"What if the laws change? Would they go along with it then?"

I remembered the 1954 Supreme Court decision giving black students the right to integrate public schools. "Some laws have changed but folks are still resisting—especially here in the South."

"Prejudice is too deep here."

Beneath his cynical expression I could see the deep hurt in his eyes. I wanted to reach out to him, to comfort him, but didn't know how. "I just wish things were different, Wally."

"Me, too, Mike."

I continued to alternate between working with Wally stacking boxes and repairing broken boxes for the rest of the summer.

More than once, Daddy said to Mama: "Gowens brags on Michael."

I guessed that Daddy was bragging on me, too, and that overall, he thought I had done a good job working at his mill and box factory that summer. That wasn't the same as him saying he was proud of me. But it was close. I so much wanted his approval. And I was glad he insisted that I work and not waste the summer loafing.

But besides pleasing Daddy, I took away the humbling experience of being accepted by and working with African Americans without the privileges of color, let alone being the boss's son. They after all worked at the mill out of necessity. The inequality of race and privilege left a lasting impression that I carried with me into college and beyond.

Acknowledgments

To my sister, Jean, and brother, Matt, for their advice, encouragement, and enthusiasm, to pursue this project. Matt's unfailing memory kept me honest with historical details. Jean enlightened the narrative with details surrounding the death of our Uncle Lionel during WWII. She also unsparingly researched and sent original prints from Mama's photo album. MotoPhoto of Bethesda, Maryland digitized the excellent images you see in the book.

Finally, my colleagues in the Bethesda Writers Group have guided my progress through this project from the very first draft to its publication. Many peer reviews helped shape the book in its final form. I am sincerely humbled by, and often in awe of, this group.

Bonnie Miller, Nancy Derr, Diana Parsell, Cheryl LaRoche, Judi Latta, Ken Ackerman, and Michael Scadron.